Exploring Home Economics
Book 1

Exploring Home Economics
Book 1

Ruth Riddell, Lorraine Scott and Lynn Rogers

Unwin Hyman

Published by
UNWIN HYMAN LIMITED
15/17 Broadwick Street
London W1V 1FP

First published in 1984 by
Longman Cheshire Pty Limited
Reprinted 1985, 1986
UK adaptation published in 1988 by
Unwin Hyman Limited
Reprinted in 1988, 1990

British Library cataloguing in Publication Data

Riddell, Ruth
   Exploring home economics.
   Book 1
   1. Home economics
   I. Title   II. Scott, Lorraine   III. Rogers, Lynn
   640   TX167

ISBN 0 7135 2792 7

Produced in Hong Kong by
L. Rex Offset Printing Co. Ltd.

Contents

Preface

Exploring Home Economics introduces the pupil to the total concept of Home Economics. The book adopts a practical approach to learning and concentrates on practical, inquiry-based exercises which encourage the pupils to make their own decisions.

The text is designed to allow schools flexibility in its use in order to meet the needs of a variety of curriculum structures. The four parts can either be taught as independent units, or used as a sequentially developed course over the period of one year.

The vocabulary is suitable for Years 1 and 2. It has been purposefully expanded as the text progresses with the intention of teaching pupils and familiarising them with the languarge of Home Economics.

Acknowledgements

The authors and publisher thank the following for permission to reproduce material supplied by them:

The Austrialian Nutrition Foundation, for their Healthy Diet Pyramid which appears on pages 44, 53, 70 and 97.

Miss B. Llewelyn, of the School of Home Economics, University College, Cardiff, for the Food Wheels System which appears on page 45.

The authors and publisher would also like to thank Miriam Staddon and Elaine Prisk of F L Calder Campus, Liverpool Polytechnic, for their help and advice in producing this book, and Angela Johnston for the photographs of kitchen utensils on pages 11, 14 and 15.

Part 1 About Home Economics

1   What is Home Economics?

Home Economics is a school subject that is about the home.

Home Economics helps you to:

- use time, energy and money wisely.............. **Management**
- prepare food... **Food Preparation**
- understand what is in food and
  how your body uses food .... **Nutrition**
- understand how people grow
  and develop.. **Human Development**
- look at the choice of places we
  have to live .... **Shelter**
- understand family living .... **Family**

In some schools the study of Textiles and Clothing is a part of Home Economics.

A Day in the Life of the Clarke Family

As you read about a morning with the Clarke family, see if you can find one example of family life to fit each area of Home Economics listed on page 2. There is more than one example for some areas.

- Make a list of your examples.

  Is your list like this one?

  Management — Mum planning to pay the bills.

  Food Preparation — Dad planning and preparing breakfast.

  Nutrition — Decisions about chocolate biscuits for lunch.

  Human Development — Daughter grown out of her jeans.

Shelter — Dad thinking the house is too small.

Family Living — Suzy asked to help Mum by bringing her washing down.

Most people in our world live in groups called families.

The Clarke family is like many other families in the world.

- Talk about the kinds of things you do in your home so that your family is fit, healthy and happy.
- Make a list of these things in your book or on the blackboard.

Home Economics helps you to develop the skills you might use in your family.

Workshop

1 In your note book write the heading **Home Economics** and in your own words write down what you think Home Economics is. This is called a **definition.**

2 Make a mobile or a display of pictures that shows what Home Economics means. (It may be helpful to read this chapter again.)

3 Hidden in the rows of jumbled letters below are 16 words related to the study of Home Economics. See if you can find them. The first one has been done to guide you.

D	A	S	T	I	M	E	R	A	H	D
Y	E	A	T	N	E	V	E	N	O	L
D	T	F	A	M	I	L	Y	Y	L	R
E	N	E	R	G	Y	R	A	E	I	N
C	G	T	E	M	O	N	E	Y	D	U
I	R	Y	S	P	L	A	N	Y	B	T
S	O	H	O	U	S	E	S	F	Y	R
I	W	U	U	R	I	T	I	O	N	I
O	T	M	R	T	H	S	C	O	L	T
N	H	O	C	H	I	R	D	D	F	I
S	S	H	E	L	T	E	R	P	U	O
L	A	P	S	C	O	O	K	T	N	N
M	A	N	A	G	E	M	E	N	T	Z

4 Match the words below with their meaning. Write the answers in your
   book.

| management | food preparation | | nutrition | human development |
| | | shelter | family | |

- understand family living
- look at the choices of places we have to live
- use time, energy and money wisely
- prepare food
- understand what is in food and how your body
  uses food
- understand how people grow and develop

2 Exploring the Home Economics Room

Where do we learn Home Economics?

Most schools have a special room for Home Economics classes. This room may look a little like your kitchen at home.
Pupils sometimes call the Home Economics Room the Cookery Room, but more than cookery happens in Home Economics classes.

Workshop

1 Draw a plan of your Home Economics Room.
2 On the plan do the following:
   a Mark the gas cookers in red.
   b Mark the electric cookers in blue.
   c Mark the refrigerators and freezers in green.

   Note: You have just used a colour code to mark the equipment in the Home Economics Room. This method of marking special items will be used in other subjects as well.

   d Mark the area where the brush and mop are kept with a cross
   e Mark the area where cleaning equipment is kept with an asterisk (*).
3 Talk about:
   "The Home Economics Room is the cleanest room in the school."
   Do you think this is so? Why?

Safety in the Home Economics Room

Each year many thousands of people are injured through accidents. Most of these accidents could be prevented. You can help prevent accidents by learning about the causes of accidents and by taking care while working. Safety in the home or the Home Economics Room is very important to you and the people around you.

- Where are the possible danger areas in the Home Economics Room?
- Make a list of these danger areas in your book.
- How many danger areas have you found?
- Compare your list with the lists made by other members of the class.

The following rules have been drawn up to help you work more safely in the Home Economics Room.

1 **Walk, Don't Run**
Can you suggest a reason for this?

2 **Beware of Spilt Food**
Why is this dangerous?

3 **Beware of Steam**
Lift the lids of saucepans, kettles, etc. so that the steam escapes away from you. Why?

4 **Be Careful with Saucepan Handles, Knives, etc.**
Do not leave saucepan handles, knives, etc. dangerously over the edge of a work surface or cooker. Why?

5 **Always Cut Away from Yourself**
Why?

There are other rules that you will learn as you work in the Room.

Workshop

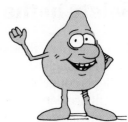

1 Where is the fire extinguisher in the Home Economics Room? Mark this on the plan you colour-coded in the last workshop.

2 In your book complete the emergency telephone number list for your family.

Emergency Telephone Numbers for the _____ **Family.**

Doctor_____	**Hospital**_____
Police_____	**Dentist**_____
Plumber _____	**Chemist**_____
Gas emergency number _____	**Veterinary Surgeon** _____
Electrician _____	

In an emergency, dial 999 for Police, Fire or Ambulance. There is no charge for a 999 call from a call box. The operator will answer by saying "Emergency, which service do you require?" She will also need to know your number and where you are calling from. Stay calm and give clear details.

3 Exploring a Recipe

Words make up the way we communicate or talk to each other.

In most subjects that you study there are special ways of using words.

Words might be used in a *special* way or have a special meaning for that subject.

A **recipe** is one way in which we communicate food preparation in Home Economics.

A recipe is a set of directions for mixing and preparing food.

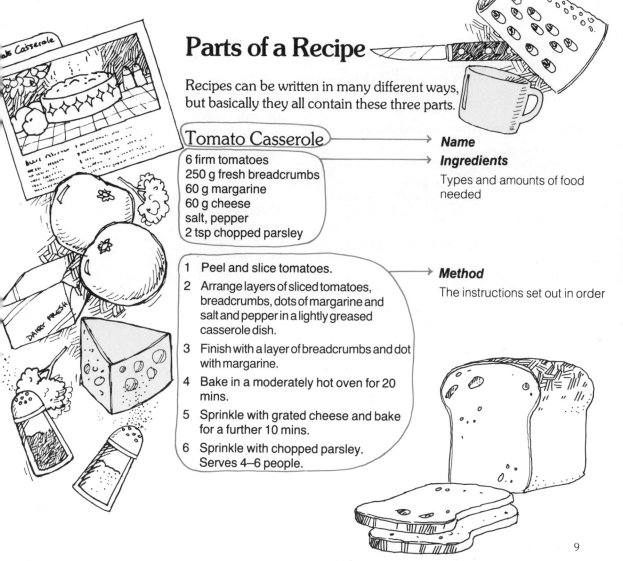

Parts of a Recipe

Recipes can be written in many different ways, but basically they all contain these three parts.

Tomato Casserole

6 firm tomatoes
250 g fresh breadcrumbs
60 g margarine
60 g cheese
salt, pepper
2 tsp chopped parsley

1   Peel and slice tomatoes.
2   Arrange layers of sliced tomatoes, breadcrumbs, dots of margarine and salt and pepper in a lightly greased casserole dish.
3   Finish with a layer of breadcrumbs and dot with margarine.
4   Bake in a moderately hot oven for 20 mins.
5   Sprinkle with grated cheese and bake for a further 10 mins.
6   Sprinkle with chopped parsley. Serves 4–6 people.

Name

Ingredients
Types and amounts of food needed

Method
The instructions set out in order

Special Words

Many of the words we use have a special meaning in food preparation.
The special words used in the Tomato Casserole recipe we have just looked at are:

peel remove the outer layer of the food.

slice cut right through the food into even-sized pieces.

chop cut up into uneven-sized pieces.

casserole food cooked in an ovenproof dish.

At the back of this book, on page 157, you will find a long list of all the special words used in this book. This list is called a **glossary.**
A glossary is a list of words with their special meaning for that subject.
Also in the Tomato Casserole recipe you might have noticed some **abbreviations** in the list of ingredients.

● What do these abbreviations mean?
The next section of this chapter will tell you the answers.

Recipe Abbreviations

An abbreviation is a shortened form of a word or some letters from a word that are used instead of the word. For example, 'Post Office' is often shortened to 'P.O.' A name like 'Timothy' may be shortened to 'Tim'.
We do the same with many words in recipes.

Some abbreviations that are used in recipes are:

kilogram	kg
gram	g
millilitre	ml
litre	l
degrees Celsius	°C
degrees Fahrenheit (on old cookers)	°F
tablespoon	tbsp
teaspoon	tsp

Oven Temperatures

Electric °C	Gas mark
140°C	1 cool
150°C	2 cool
160°C	3 moderate
180°C	4 moderate
190°C	5 fairly hot
200°C	6 fairly hot
220°C	7 hot
230°C	8 very hot

Measurement

The careful measurement of your foods should help you to be successful with your recipes. The picture to the right shows measuring equipment used in a kitchen.
Your teacher will show you the correct way to use this equipment.

Workshop

1   What are the *abbreviations* for the following measures used in recipes? Write the abbreviations in your book.

Measure	Abbreviation
teaspoon	_____
tablespoon	_____
litre	_____
gram	_____
millilitre	_____
kilogram	_____

YOU DECIDE!

2   How can you work out the equivalent measure for each of the following measures? Write the equivalent measures in your book.

Measure		Equivalent Measure
1 tablespoon	=	_____ teaspoons
1 litre	=	_____ pints
1 kilogram	=	_____ grams
1 litre	=	_____ millilitres
1 pint	=	_____ millilitres

3   Collect a number of magazines that have recipes in them. Select 5 recipes. Mark any of the words in the recipes that you do not understand. Look them up in the glossary at the back of this book. If they are not there, how can you find out what they mean?
When you have found out the meanings, start your own glossary at the back of your note book. Add to your glossary as you find new Home Economics words.

4   Work your way through the following practical exercise.

Practical Exercise No. 1
Equipment

Aims

- To help me to remember where the equipment is in the Home Economics Room
- To practise measuring ingredients accurately

Procedure

a Collect a tray from your teacher.

b Collect the following items from their storage place and put them on the tray.

rolling pin	spatula	fork
measuring jug	peeler	small basin
chopping board	grater	whisk
cook's knife		

c Ask your teacher to check that you have all the pieces of equipment. Return equipment to correct storage place.

d Correctly measure 200 ml of water, 100 g of sugar and 1¼ tbsp of flour. Your teacher will check that you have done this correctly by using a checklist like the one below:

Checklist for Activity d

	yes	no
— Selects the correct dry or liquid measuring equipment	____	____
— Selects the correct size equipment	____	____
— Is able to use scales and weigh accurately	____	____
— Checks liquid measures correctly at eye level	____	____
— Measures in such a way that no ingredient is spilled on the table or floor.	____	____

5 Now that you know how to read a recipe and how to measure ingredients, prepare a recipe in which you need to use scales, spoons and measuring jugs to measure dry and liquid ingredients. A recipe is suggested here. Your teacher might suggest a different one.

Recipes to Try

Chocolate Crispies

Ingredients

50 g wholewheat flakes
2 tsps cocoa
25 g sugar
25 g margarine
1 tbsp golden syrup
1 tbsp coconut
25 g currants

Method

1 Heat a mixing bowl under a hot tap. Empty and dry, then put in the sugar, margarine and syrup.

2 Place carefully in a larger bowl of hot water to come ½ way up the mixing bowl.

3 Stir, mixing thoroughly until the margarine has melted. Stir in the cocoa.

4 Stir in wholewheat flakes, coconut and currants and mix until coated.

5 Spoon mixture into paper cake cases and leave to set.

This recipe makes 8 - 10 cakes.

Questions about the recipe

a What is the correct way to measure a teaspoon of cocoa?

b Why should you use a warmed spoon to measure the syrup?

c The margarine sugar and syrup should not be boiled, why?

d Make a list of the different methods of measuring you used when making this recipe.

4 Exploring Equipment

Equipment in the Home Economics Room can be divided into three groups:

Small Equipment: These are things like spoons, bowls, knives and whisks. They are called **utensils**. Any one utensil has many uses, for example, a fork might be used to whip an egg, to make holes in pastry, to eat with or to pick up pieces of food.

Small Appliances: These are small and movable, for example, electric mixers.
• See how many other small appliances your class can think of.

Large Appliances: These are very large and are not usually moved.
• What large appliances does your Home Economics Room have?

Small Equipment

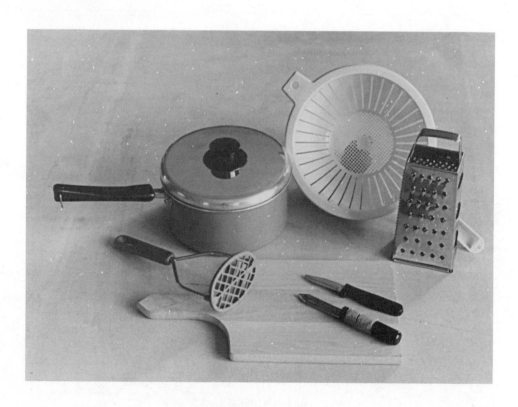

Small Equipment Workshop

The three groups of equipment shown here have been collected by pupils in preparation for their practical work.

1 List the equipment in each group and give one use for each piece of equipment.
2 What do you think each pupil may be making?

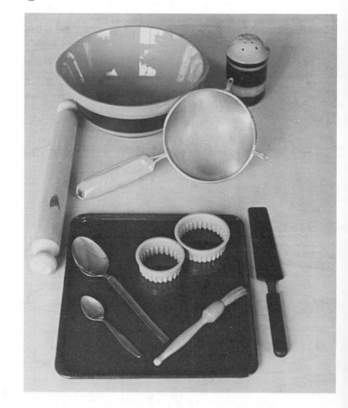

15

3   Sean's mother has asked him to mash the potatoes. Look carefully at the pictures of utensils on page 15 and list all the things he could use.

4   Sufia wishes to take sausages from the grill tray. What could she use to do this safely?

5   Complete the puzzle with the names of the equipment.

DOWN

ACROSS

YOU DECIDE!

6 Work your way through the following practical exercise.

Practical Exercise No. 2
Using Utensils

Aims

- To learn how to use some of the equipment in the Home Economics Room
- To discover that any one utensil has many uses

Procedure

a Watch your teacher as you are shown how to prepare the Traffic Light Sandwich recipe at the end of this workshop, or a similar recipe requiring a variety of utensils.

b List each of the utensils you used to prepare your recipe down the left-hand side of your page. Write next to each utensil what you used it for in the recipe, and suggest one other use for that utensil in food preparation.

Example

Name of each utensil used to make traffic light sandwiches	What did you use the utensil for?	What else could that utensil be used for in food preparation?
an apple corer	making holes in bread	coring apples

7 Watch as your teacher shows you how to **shred, dice, finely chop, slice** and **grate** the ingredients in the Coleslaw recipe at the end of this workshop, or a similar recipe using a number of food preparation skills.

Recipes to Try

Traffic Light Sandwiches

Ingredients

2 slices of wholemeal bread
Butter to spread on one slice of the bread
(30g of butter can be shared among four
pupils)
1–2 tsp cheese spread
*1 small piece of carrot
 1 slice of tomato
 a piece of green lettuce leaf

*Any other foods can be used, as long as you have red,
orange and green colours.

Method

1 Using a **round bladed knife**, spread one
   slice of bread with butter.

2 Take an **apple corer** and make holes in
   the buttered bread like this:

(Check size of corer to make sure 9 holes
 fit on the slice of bread.)

3 Using a round bladed knife, spread the
   other slice of bread with cheese spread.

4 Cut a slice of tomato with a **serrated knife,**
   then cut the slice in two.

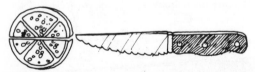

5 Grate a small piece of carrot using the
   big cutting side of a **grater.**

6 Place the fillings carefully on top of the
   cheese spread.

7 Now place the slice with the holes
   carefully over these fillings with the
   buttered side next to the filling.

8 Put your sandwich on a **chopping board**
   and cut it into three strips with a **cook's
   knife** so that you have the colours for
   'stop', 'caution' and 'go' on each strip.

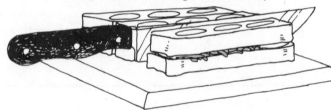

9 Serve neatly on a plate with a paper doily.

10 Wash up all your equipment and put it
    away correctly. Wipe the work surface
    clean.

Traffic Light Sandwiches are fun to serve at a
party.

Coleslaw

Ingredients

¼ small cabbage
½ carrot
½ green pepper
½ onion
1 stick celery
½ apple
4 tbsps French dressing or mayonnaise

Method

1 Wash and dry all vegetables.

2 Shred cabbage (cut cabbage finely with a knife).

3 Grate carrot.

4 Dice apple (cut into cubes).

5 Slice celery and green pepper.

6 Finely chop up onion.

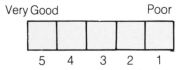

7 Mix together in a bowl.

8 Add French dressing.

9 Serve salad on a plate with a slice of meat, a hard boiled egg or a slice of cheese; fill into a wholemeal bread roll to make a salad sandwich or take home in a jar to have with your dinner.

Questions about the recipe

a What do the following cookery terms mean? Write the meaning for each term in your book.

shred   grate   dice   slice   chop

b Complete this sentence in your book: French dressing is a mixture of o____ and v____ and is used to give flavour to the salad.

c List 4 foods you could serve with coleslaw.

d How do you rate your salad? Copy the scale below into your book and put a tick in one of the boxes.

Very Good				Poor
5	4	3	2	1

Small Appliances

Many appliances have been developed to do kitchen tasks. They have been designed to save time. They can do all sorts of things from boiling water to cooking a dinner slowly.

The people who make these products usually supply books with them. These books explain how to use the appliances. To make sure your applicances work well you should follow the instructions carefully.

You should only use an appliance for the purpose for which it was designed.

Take care with electricity. Make sure the current is switched off before cleaning your appliance.

Workshop

1   Collect as many pictures of small appliances as you can find. Make a display of them on the board in your classroom.

2   **Class Survey:**   One way of finding out something is to conduct a **survey.** In a survey you ask a number of people the same questions. You then add up your answers. This gives you your results.

The group of people in your survey is called a **sample** of the population. Use your class as a sample and conduct the survey in the following practical exercise.

Practical Exercise No. 3
Small Appliances

Aim

● To discover the number and types of small appliances in the home

Procedure

a   Plan a survey sheet similar to the one below.

Appliance Survey

At home you have a number of small appliances. Place a tick in the box below for each of the small appliances you have at home.

Toaster	☐	Coffee Maker	☐
Electric Frying Pan	☐	Deep Fat Fryer	☐
Electric Jug Kettle	☐	Food Processor	☐
Electric Mixer	☐	Sandwich Toaster	☐

Others ....

(List any other small appliances you may have at home.)

---

b   Ask each member of your class to fill in the survey sheet.

c   With your teacher's help count up the number of pupils that have each of the above small appliances at home. Record them on a result sheet similar to the one below:

Results

Number of people in class ☐

Appliance	Total
Toaster	
Electric Frying Pan	
Electric Jug Kettle	
Electric Mixer	
Coffee Maker	
Deep Fat Fryer	
Food Processor	
Sandwich Toaster	

Others (continue list)

d   Now answer these questions in your book:

— The most popular appliance is ....

— ....% of the class owns one. (Ask your teacher to show you how to work out percentage (%).)

— The average number of appliances in the homes of members of this class is .... (Ask your teacher to show you how to work out a class average.)

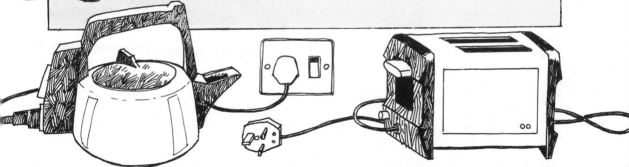

Large Appliances

Cookers

A large amount of the food we eat is cooked. In the kitchen food is usually cooked on a cooker, or on a small appliance that has been designed for a specific purpose such as deep frying. Most kitchens have a cooker.

The heat for the cooker is usually provided by two main sources:

- gas
- electricity

The normal family cooker has three parts:

Sometimes these parts are put together as one large piece of equipment or they may be divided up into two or three parts.

Example:

The hob can be fitted into the work top, while the oven can be fitted into a wall. Each part of the cooker is suitable for a different cooking method.

Hob or Hotplates

Grill

Oven

The **hob** can be used for:

- boiling food in liquid
- steaming food over water
- frying food in oil or fat
- stewing food slowly in a small quantity of liquid with the lid on.

Control knobs for each ring or burner allow you to turn the heat up or down.

The **grill** can give out very rapid heat to cook food quickly; but the heat can be turned down if you wish.

The **oven** is used for baking, roasting and for casseroles as well as for heating food. Gas ovens and electric ovens are a little different in the way they can be used.

Because of the high temperatures that are created when cooking care must always be taken.

Each part of the cooker has its own special safety needs. These should be studied carefully before using it.

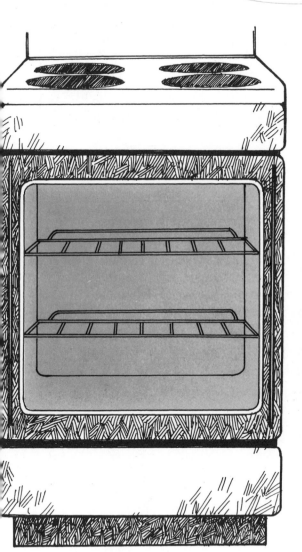

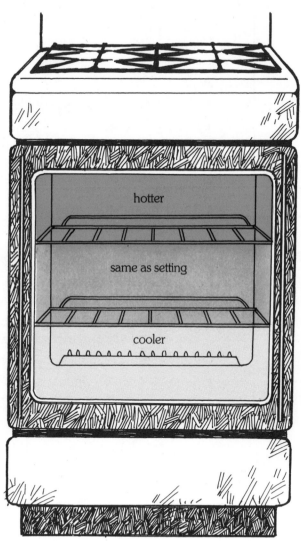

In an *electric oven* the heat comes from elements along the sides of the oven. There are only slight differences in the temperatures between the top and bottom of the oven.

Some electric cookers are fitted with fans which circulate the heat around the oven and so the heat in the oven is even. These are called fan assisted ovens.

A *gas oven* has three *zones of heat*. The number on the dial is the heat at the centre of the oven. Because hot air rises, the top of the oven is hotter and the bottom of the oven is cooler.

Workshop

1 Work your way through *the next four practical exercises* to earn your
cooker licence.

Practical Exercise No. 4
Using the Oven

Aims

- To use the oven of a gas or electric cooker safely and efficiently
- To use the basic cookery method of baking
- To learn the cooking terms: **rubbing in, knead, dough, glaze**

Procedure

a Read through the recipe you are to prepare (we suggest the **Scones**
recipe at the end of this workshop).

b Look carefully at the oven temperature required. Which shelf should
you use in your oven to bake the recipe at the required temperature?
Look back to p. 23 if you need help. Arrange the oven shelves in
the correct postion. Light the oven and set the thermostat.

c Collect your ingredients and prepare the recipe after your teacher has
demonstrated it and explained each part of the method to you.

d Answer the questions at the end of the recipe.

e Turn the oven off when it is no longer needed.

Practical Exercise No. 5
Using the Hotplates

Aims

- To cook a simple meal using the hotplates or burners of a cooker
- To learn how to use the hotplates or burners
- To put into practice safety procedures to be used when cooking on hotplates or burners

Procedure

a Before starting to cook discuss:

— How should the saucepan handle be placed when you put the saucepan on the hob? Why?

— How should the lid be removed from a steaming saucepan? Why?

— If gas does not light automatically (without a match), should you turn on the gas first, or light the match first? Why?

— What would you do if oil in a pan caught fire?

b Now make up the recipe for this lesson (we suggest the **Fried Rice** recipe at the end of this workshop).

c Answer the questions at the end of the recipe.

Practical Exercise No. 6
Using the Grill

Aims

- To cook a simple meal using the grill
- To learn how to use the grill of the gas or electric cooker
- To put into practice safety precautions that are necessary when using the grill

Procedure

a Before starting to cook discuss:

— Should the door of the grill be open or closed when being used. Why?

— How can food be put on and removed from the grill tray?

b Prepare the suggested recipe for yourself. (We suggest the **Spring Morning Breakfast** recipe at the end of this workshop.)

c Answer the questions at the end of the recipe.

Practical Exercise No. 7
Final Licence Test

Aim

- To demonstrate my understanding of the use of cookers.

Procedure

a **Electric Cooker**

— Turn the heat on the *left back hotplate* to 'High'. On the hotplate place a saucepan with 250 ml of water in it. Bring the water to the boil. When it is boiling have it checked by your teacher. Now bring the water down to a simmer.

Checked ....
(Signature of tester)

— Switch the grill on to 'Medium'.

Checked ....
(Signature of tester)

– Switch the oven on to 200°C.

Checked ....
(Signature of tester)

b **Gas Cooker**

— Light the *right front burner* and turn it to 'High'. On the burner place a saucepan with 250 ml of water in it. Bring the water to the boil. When it is boiling have it checked by your teacher. Now bring the water down to a simmer.

Checked ....
(Signature of tester)

— Light the grill and switch it on to 'Medium'.

Checked ....
(Signature of tester)

— Light the oven and set it on to mark 5.

Checked ....
(Signature of tester)

Recipes to Try

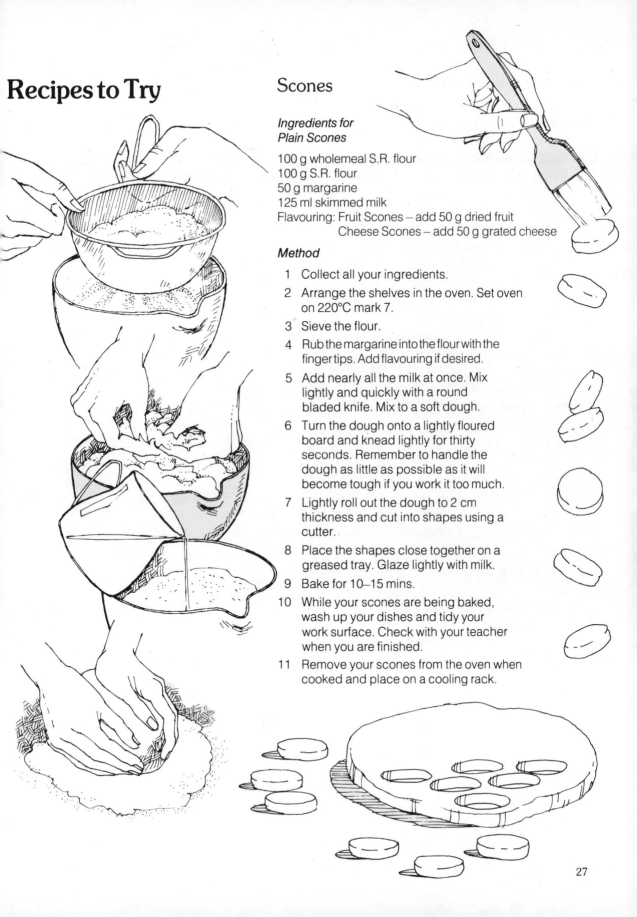

Scones

Ingredients for Plain Scones

100 g wholemeal S.R. flour
100 g S.R. flour
50 g margarine
125 ml skimmed milk
Flavouring: Fruit Scones – add 50 g dried fruit
                Cheese Scones – add 50 g grated cheese

Method

1 Collect all your ingredients.

2 Arrange the shelves in the oven. Set oven on 220°C mark 7.

3 Sieve the flour.

4 Rub the margarine into the flour with the finger tips. Add flavouring if desired.

5 Add nearly all the milk at once. Mix lightly and quickly with a round bladed knife. Mix to a soft dough.

6 Turn the dough onto a lightly floured board and knead lightly for thirty seconds. Remember to handle the dough as little as possible as it will become tough if you work it too much.

7 Lightly roll out the dough to 2 cm thickness and cut into shapes using a cutter.

8 Place the shapes close together on a greased tray. Glaze lightly with milk.

9 Bake for 10–15 mins.

10 While your scones are being baked, wash up your dishes and tidy your work surface. Check with your teacher when you are finished.

11 Remove your scones from the oven when cooked and place on a cooling rack.

Questions about the recipe

Choose the correct answers to questions 'a' to 'e'.

a Which of the following *is not* a reason for sifting flour?
— To remove air from flour
— To put air into the flour
— To mix the dry ingredients together
— To remove lumps from the flour

b The tips of the fingers are used to rub margarine into flour because:
— they are the hottest part of the hands and will melt the butter
— they are coolest part of the hands and will not melt the butter
— they are the cleanest part of the hands and will not discolour the flour.

c The scone dough is kneaded for
— 30 seconds
— 60 seconds
— 90 seconds.

d When you use the oven you should always arrange the oven shelves
— before switching on the oven
— after switching on the oven
— during cooking.

e The best way to remove a hot tray from the oven is
— with a wet cloth
— with a synthetic cloth
— with oven gloves made from natural fibres, *e.g.* cotton, wool.

f In your book, match the terms with the correct definitions.

Rubbing in   Knead   Dough   Glaze

● To work a dough lightly with the hands until smooth

● A mixture of flour and a liquid

● A liquid brushed over the surface of some foods before baking to improve the appearance

● To rub fat or margarine into flour with the tips of the fingers

g Why did your scones increase in size?

h How can you tell when your scones are cooked?

Fried Rice

Ingredients

1 litre water
¼ tsp salt
100 g rice
1 tbsp oil
1 spring onion
50 g mushrooms
1 egg
25 g green pepper

Method

1 Boil water and salt. Add rice and boil for 12 mins (25 mins for brown rice).

2 Drain through a colander.

3 Spread out on a tray to cool and dry.

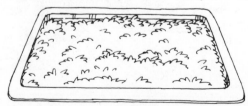

4 Wash and chop all vegetables finely. Beat egg with a fork.

5 Heat oil in pan or wok. Add egg. When set, remove from pan and slice up. Add vegetables and stir for 3–4 mins.

6 Add rice and stir fry until a little brown. Add 1 tsp soy sauce if you like. Stir egg back into rice. Serves 2–3.

Questions about the recipe

a What is the difference between boiling water and simmering water?

b List the equipment used in the recipe.

c How do you rate your Fried Rice? Copy the scale below into your book and put a tick in one of the boxes.

Very Good   Poor

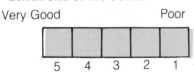

5	4	3	2	1

d What else could you add to the Fried Rice?

e If you did not like this dish, give your reasons.

Spring Morning Breakfast

Ingredients

1 slice of bread
1 slice of Cheddar cheese
1 slice of tomato
1 slice of ham
1 sprig of parsley

Method

1 Switch on or light grill
2 Toast one side of the bread until light brown.
3 Place ham on the untoasted side of bread.
4 Add cheese.
5 Place tomato on top.
6 Grill till cheese is golden in colour.
7 Place on a plate.
8 Garnish (decorate) with parsley.
Serves 1.

Questions about the recipe

a What equipment did you use?

b Describe what happens when cheese is placed under the grill.

c How long did the recipe take to prepare?

d What does 'garnish' mean?

e How can you design your own breakfast using cheese and bread as a start? Write out your recipe. Give your recipe a name.

● Your class could make their own QUICK BREAKFASTS RECIPE BOOK. It could be printed and sold to raise money for charity.

Microwave Ovens

How Microwaves Work

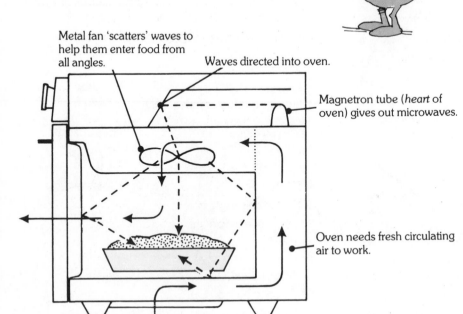

Metal fan 'scatters' waves to help them enter food from all angles.

Waves directed into oven.

Magnetron tube (*heart* of oven) gives out microwaves.

Oven needs fresh circulating air to work.

KEY

- - - → Microwaves

——→ Air

Waves go straight through container — metal must not be used or waves might be bounced back into magnetron and damage it (this is called *arcing*). Use china, glass or plastic containers with NO metallic decoration. [Some ovens allow metal utensils — read manufacturer's instructions carefully.]

Waves *bounce* off metal walls of oven, they enter food anything from 1–9 cm (never more than) and make the tiny particles (*molecules*) of water vibrate. Vibration causes heat; food cooks. Food does not brown unless oven has a special browning dish or browner.

Using the Oven

1 Read the manufacturer's instructions carefully

2 The oven can be used for
   - thawing food
   - reheating cooked food
   - cooking food.

Workshop

1 If you cooked meat in a microwave without a browning dish or browner, to save time how could you brown it quickly if you also had an ordinary cooker?

2 Scrub two potatoes of the same size ready for baking in their jackets. Preheat a gas or an electric oven on 200°C, mark 6. Place one potato in the ordinary oven and *at the same time* place the other in the microwave using the setting suggested in the instruction book. Then answer these questions:
   a How long did each potato take to cook?
   b How much time was saved using the microwave?
   c Examine both potatoes; record any differences you can see.
   d *Without* adding anything to the potatoes, taste them both. Was there any difference in the flavour?

Discuss your observations with the rest of the class.

YOU DECIDE!

Recipe to Try

Date and Walnut Loaf

Ingredients

100 g chopped dates
50 g finely chopped walnuts
100 g sugar
20 g margarine
1 tsp bicarbonate of soda
¼ tsp ground mixed spice
225 g S.R. flour
250 ml boiling water

Method

1 Place all ingredients **except** the flour and water into a bowl.
2 Pour in the boiling water and mix well until the margarine melts.
3 Fold in flour and pour the mixture into a greased pyrex 25 × 10 cm loaf dish.
4 Cover with plastic wrap and cook for approximately 5 mins depending on type of microwave used. Check instruction book.
5 Remove cover. Allow to stand in dish for 3 minutes then turn onto a cooling rack.

Refrigerators and Freezers

Refrigerators are important for keeping food fresh. Different foods keep for different amounts of time in the refrigerator; for example, a jar of mayonnaise will keep for about 2 months while fresh milk will only keep for a few days.

Food stored in the refrigerator should be covered as this stops loss of water from the food.

Covering food also stops strong odours like those from fish and onion affecting the taste of all foods in the refrigerator.

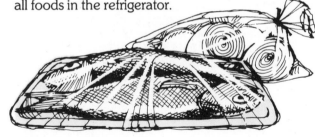

Freezers keep foods frozen. They may be found at the top of a refrigerator, they may look the same as a refrigerator, or they may be a chest type appliance.

Temperatures in freezers should be –18°C or lower to keep food frozen and safe.

Doors of freezers should be opened as little as possible to prevent loss of temperature.

Workshop

1 a   To find out the temperature in the refrigerator at school, place a thermometer on the refrigerator shelf and record the temperature.

   b   Do the same for the freezer. What is the difference in temperature?

Which of these appliances would keep food for the longer period of time?

2   Copy the diagram of the refrigerator into your book. On the diagram label the types of foods you would store in each section.

3   Complete the crossword.

Clues
Across

3 Salad .... are stored in the salad drawer.
8 Never put ...... food in the refrigerator.
9 Refrigerators are important for keeping food ....
10 Some refrigerators are now .... automatically

Down
1   .... is made in the frozen food compartment.
2   .... is usually stored in bottles or cartons in the door.
4   .... are stored in a special rack in the door.
5 These and other meat products should be stored in the coldest part of the fridge.
6 Use the frozen food compartment to make your own ice .... (use pure fruit juice).
7 Food should always be .... before being stored in the refrigerator.

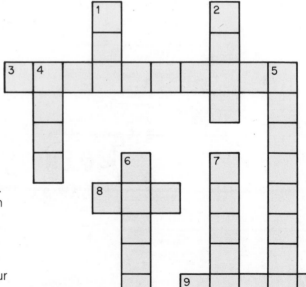

5 Keeping Clean

As food is handled in the Home Economics Room, it is important to make sure that all equipment and work areas are kept very clean, and that the people working in the Room are also clean.

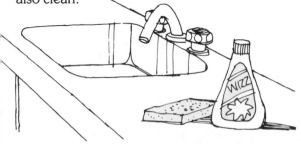

The greatest enemies of the Home Economics Room and of the home kitchen are bacteria (often called germs). Bacteria are extremely small, too small to be seen without a microscope.

• Do you know what a microscope is and what it is used for?

Four hundred million (400,000,000) bacteria clumped together will only look as big as a grain of sugar. (Look at a grain of sugar and remember its size.)

Bacteria can grow very quickly on food. If you eat food with large numbers of harmful bacteria on it you may become ill (food poisoning).

• Let us keep our food clean by following these rules:

Ten Golden Rules for Safe Food Preparation

1 Wash hands before starting to prepare food and after touching bacteria breeding areas (toilet, refuse, soil, raw meat, handkerchief).

2 Make sure all equipment, work surfaces, sinks and floor are clean.

3 Wear clean protective clothing.

4 Tie back long hair.

5 Cover any sores, cuts or wounds.

6 Keep food and equipment protected from flies and rodents (rats and mice).

7 Keep foods that go bad easily (i.e. perishables) in the refrigerator.

8 Do not prepare food for others if you are not well.

9 Do not lick your fingers while preparing food.

10 Do not replace the tasting spoon in food after use.

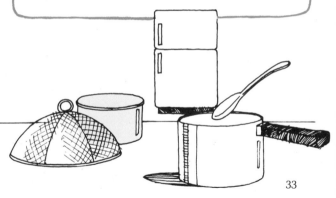

Workshop

1 What do we mean by **perishable** foods?

2 Why are the ten golden rules for safe food preparation important?

3 Work your way through the following practical exercises to help you to work hygienically.

Practical Exercise No. 8
Keeping Equipment Clean

Aim

● To discover and use the correct method for washing dishes by hand *(This is part of golden rule no. 2)*

Procedure

a Prepare the recipe at the end of this workshop or one decided on by your teacher.

b Serve the meal and keep it warm in a very slow oven.

c Scrape all your dishes and sort them into piles — according to how dirty they are.

d Half fill your sink with hot water and add 2 teaspoons of detergent. *(Be accurate; this is an experiment.)*

e Wash your dishes. Save 1 glass full of the washing-up water. Then empty the sink and sit down to eat your meal.

f When you have finished eating, scrape the dishes.

g Half fill the sink again with hot water and add two teaspoons of detergent. Wash your dishes thoroughly. Save a glass of the washing-up water before emptying the sink.

h Stir up the first glass of water and compare the two.

i Which was the dirtier glass of washing-up water?

j In which order should dishes be washed?

k Give reasons for your decision.

Recipes to Try

Tomato Meat Balls

Ingredients

225 g lean minced beef
½ grated onion
½ grated apple
pinch curry powder
pinch salt
250 ml tomato soup
125 ml water
2 tbsps flour
50 g grated cheese

Method

1 Mix all ingredients except tomato soup, water, flour and cheese.

2 Shape the mixture into 8 or 12 balls.

3 Roll in flour.

4 Heat tomato soup and water in a saucepan and bring to the boil.

5 Place meatballs in soup mixture and simmer for 30 mins.

6 Serve 2–3 meatballs in a small dish and sprinkle with cheese. Serves 4.

• This recipe could be served with cooked pasta.

To cook pasta

a Weigh 50g pasta for each person.

b Half fill a large saucepan with hot water. Add ½ tsp salt. ·

c Bring the water to the boil, add the pasta and stir once or twice.

d Simmer for 15–20 mins until tender.

e Drain through colander.

35

Part 1   Evaluation Test

Work your way through the following evaluation test.

1   In your book, match the terms with the definitions.

**Ingredient   Method
Palette Knife   Recipe   Grater**

- A flexible blunt knife.
- Directions, including list of food items required for preparing a dish.
- Food item in a recipe.
- Used to cut food into small pieces quickly.
- Detailed steps of how to prepare a recipe.

2   In your book, match the mixing methods with the correct definitions.

Rubbing in   Knead   Sift   Stir

- Rub butter/margarine into flour with the tips of the fingers.
- Work a flour mixture by hand until a smooth dough is formed.
- Put dry ingredients through a sieve or sifter to remove lumps and to add air.
- Mix ingredients with a circular motion.

3   Describe what the following items would look like.
- Diced carrot
- Shredded lettuce
- Grated apple

4   In your book, match the cooking terms with their definitions.

**Boiling point   Casserole   Brown   Freeze
Garnish   Simmer**

- Decoration for food.
- Water reaches this point at 100°C.
- Food cooked in the oven in an ovenproof dish with a lid.
- Make food brown in colour by frying, grilling, toasting or baking.
- Make food cold and hard.
- Bring a liquid to a temperature just below boiling point.

5 In your book, write the abbreviations for the weights,
   measures, time and oven temperature listed below.

   gram   ....
   kilogram   ....
   degrees celsius ....
   minutes   ....
   millilitre   ....
   litre   ....
   tablespoon   ....
   teaspoon   ....

6 Match the oven temperatures with the terms which are often
   used in recipes. Write them in your book, and add the gas mark.

Hot	Cool	Moderate	Gas mark
....	200°C	....
....	150°C	....
....	180°C	....

7 Arrange the following steps into an order that should assist you to be
   successful with a recipe.

   Measure exactly.
   Read recipe carefully.
   Mix carefully.
   Collect utensils.
   Collect ingredients.
   Set oven temperature.
   Bake or cook as directed.
   Complete preparation of ingredients.

8 Write out one of the golden rules for safe food preparation and explain
   how it helps us to keep food clean and safe.

9 Look back at the safety rules on page 7. How many more safety rules
   did you learn in Part 1 of this book?

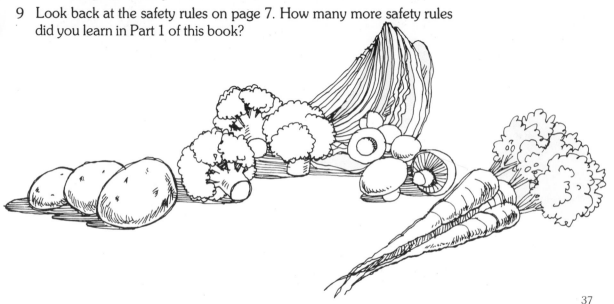

An extra puzzle for you

Hidden in the letter maze are fifteen pieces of equipment that we often use in the Home Economics Room.

Give yourself ten minutes and see how many you can find.

The words may go across the page, that is, horizontally; up and down, that is, vertically; and from one corner to the other, that is, diagonally.

List the words in your book as you find them. The first one has been done to guide you.

F	O	R	K	T	L	M	G	U	X	Y	F
S	P	O	O	N	O	A	R	I	E	T	R
P	U	W	W	I	I	R	A	C	U	P	E
A	E	O	H	H	D	F	T	U	L	A	E
T	R	E	V	I	I	K	E	T	H	N	Z
U	S	L	L	E	S	S	R	T	O	T	E
L	O	N	T	E	N	Z	K	E	W	T	R
A	P	A	S	T	R	Y	B	R	U	S	H
T	B	G	R	J	K	Q	R	Y	U	O	P

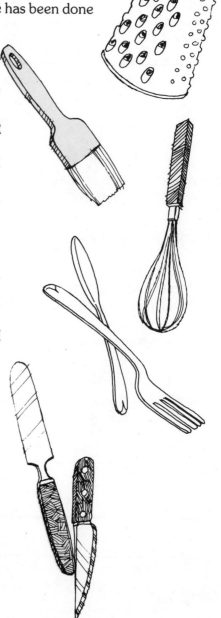

Part 2   About Food

6   Introducing Food

Food and You

Cars, like people, come in all shapes and sizes.

To function properly, cars need fuel. Fuel consists of a lot of petrol, a moderate amount of oil and a little grease.

People, too, need fuel to function. Our fuel needs are met by **food**.

Our fuel consists of:
- foods which we need the **most** of, such as bread, cereals, fruit and vegetables.

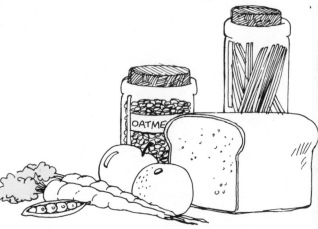

- foods that we need a **moderate** amount of, such as milk, cheese and yoghurt, meat, eggs and poultry, nuts and pulses.

- foods we need the **least** of, such as butter, margarine, oil and sugar.

Both cars and people also need water, to help their systems function. Petrol, oil, grease and water all have a specific function in a car.

Similarly, food has specific substances that it must supply the body with so that all parts of the body work properly.

A petrol station supplies all the car's needs and we know when the car is low on petrol. We have our cars checked regularly to see that they have oil and water. They are serviced regularly and topped up with little extras like brake fluid, grease, etc.

We are not so lucky with our bodies. We do not have a gauge to tell us when we are empty or full. Our choice of food is very wide. We do not come with a set of specific instructions to tell us what types of foods we need and when we need them.

Workshop

1 Discuss
    - How do you know when you are hungry?
    - How do you know when you have had enough to eat?
    - How do you know you have eaten the foods your body needs?
2 Keep a record of the foods you eat in one day. Compare this with the records kept by other members of the class. Discuss why people eat different kinds of foods and in different amounts.

Food and Your Body

Did you know?

- **Nutrition** is the study of how the body uses food.

- **Nutritionists** are people who study nutrition.

- **Nutrients** are complex chemical substances that are found in food. The body needs them to carry out all its functions and to stay healthy.

- **Diet** is the name for the food we eat each day. It is not, as many people think, related to food we eat when we want to lose weight. That is a special diet, and should be called a *reducing* diet.

- **A Dietician** is a person who has studied nutrition and who advises people about their diets. A dietician usually works in a hospital.

- **A Healthy Diet** is a diet that contains all the nutrients the body needs. These nutrients are obtained by eating a *variety* of foods.

- **Vegetarians** do not eat meat; some do not eat any animal products at all. With careful food choice all the body's needs can be met.

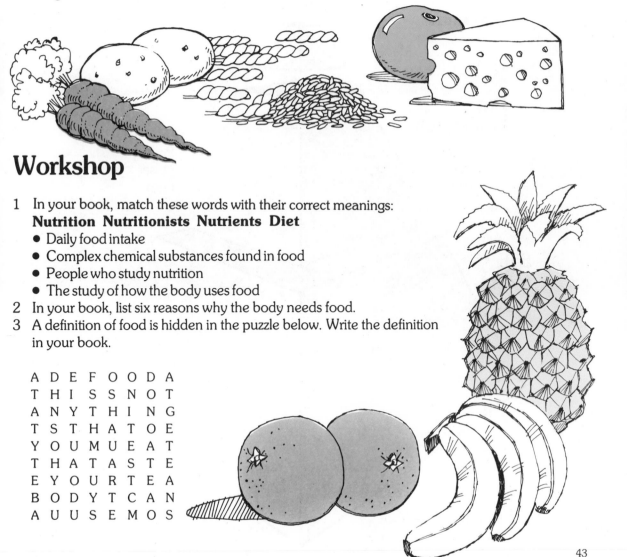

Workshop

1   In your book, match these words with their correct meanings:
Nutrition Nutritionists Nutrients Diet
- Daily food intake
- Complex chemical substances found in food
- People who study nutrition
- The study of how the body uses food
2   In your book, list six reasons why the body needs food.
3   A definition of food is hidden in the puzzle below. Write the definition in your book.

```
A  D  E  F  O  O  D  A
T  H  I  S  S  N  O  T
A  N  Y  T  H  I  N  G
T  S  T  H  A  T  O  E
Y  O  U  M  U  E  A  T
T  H  A  T  A  S  T  E
E  Y  O  U  R  T  E  A
B  O  D  Y  T  C  A  N
A  U  U  S  E  M  O  S
```

Deciding What to Eat

Many ways have been developed to help us decide which foods we should eat. Below are three ways that could be used. It is important that you should select a way of choosing food that suits **you**.

The Healthy Diet Pyramid

Tells us the proportion of food we should eat.

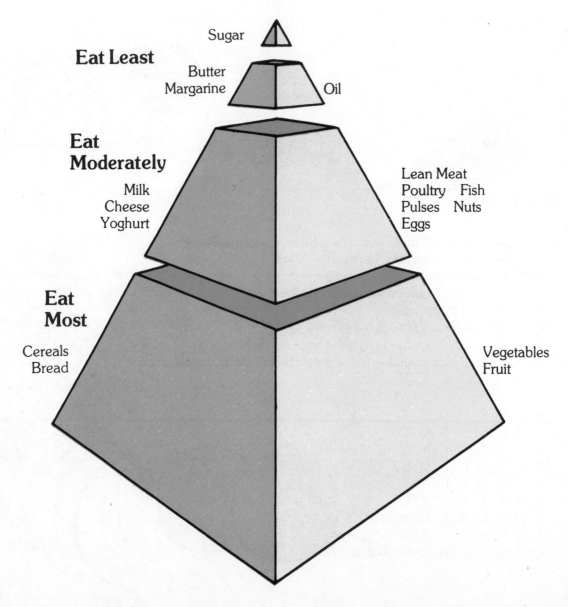

Eat Least

Sugar

Butter
Margarine   Oil

Eat Moderately

Milk
Cheese
Yoghurt

Lean Meat
Poultry   Fish
Pulses   Nuts
Eggs

Eat Most

Cereals
Bread

Vegetables
Fruit

The Food Wheels System

Also tells us which foods are
important to eat.

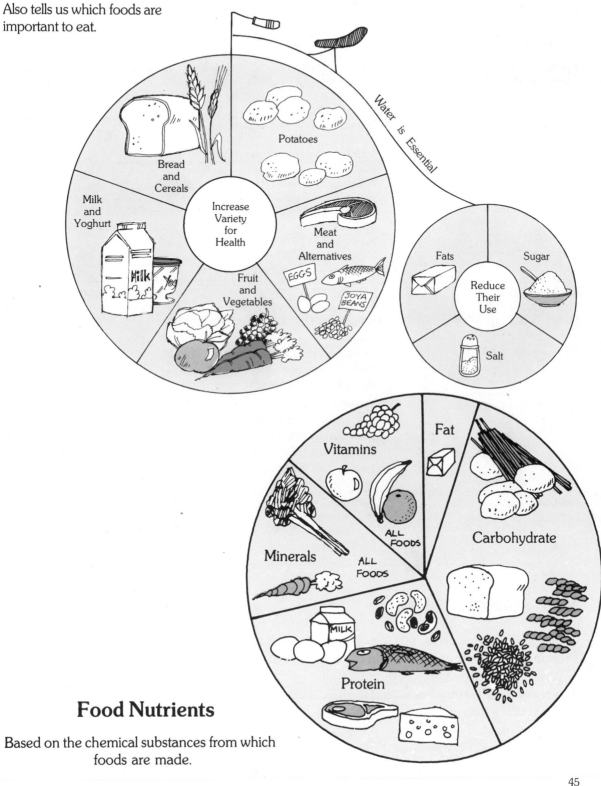

Food Nutrients

Based on the chemical substances from which
foods are made.

The Food Nutrients, the Food Wheels System and the Healthy Diet Pyramid all suggest that we should eat a **variety** of foods each day. They also suggest an order of importance for food choices.

Healthy Diet Pyramid	Food Nutrients	The Food Wheels System
Eat Most Cereals and Bread	**Carbohydrates** ● For energy ● Fibre for eliminating waste from your body **Vitamin A** for healthy skin and eyes	**Increase Variety for Health** Bread and Cereals
Fruit and Vegetables	**Vitamin C** to protect body from infection **B Group Vitamins** for healthy nerves and for getting energy from the 'Eat Most' foods **Minerals** ● *Calcium* and *Phosphorus* for healthy bones and teeth ● *Iron* for healthy blood	Potatoes Fruit and Vegetables
Eat Moderately Meat, Poultry, Fish Pulses, Nuts, Eggs Milk, Cheese, Yoghurt	**Protein** ● For growth and repair of body tissue **Minerals** ● *Calcium* and *Phosphorus* for healthy bones and teeth ● *Iron* for healthy blood **Vitamins** ● **A** for healthy skin and eyes **B** for healthy nerves and getting energy from 'Eat Most' foods **Fats** for heat and energy	Meat and Alternatives Milk and Yoghurt
Eat Least Butter, Margarine, Sugar	**Fats and Oils** ● For energy **Vitamins** A, D, E, K **Carbohydrate** only	**Reduce Their Use** Fats, Sugar, Salt

Workshop

1 In your book, match the nutrients to their body functions.
Protein   Carbohydrate   Vitamin A   Iron   Calcium   Fat

- A rich source of energy
- Necessary for healthy bones and teeth
- For building new cells
- Provides energy
- For healthy skin and eyes
- For healthy blood

2   Look carefully at the list of foods below.
Butter, wholemeal bread, margarine, lettuce, apples, cream, steak,
cheese, eggs, bacon, milk, tomatoes, cucumber, honey, sugar, golden
syrup, brown rice, potatoes, chick peas, muesli, lentils

Rule up a table like the one below and write the foods in the
appropriate column.

'Eat Most' group	'Eat Moderately' group	'Eat Least' group

3   Plan a healthy diet for yourself for one day. Include breakfast, lunch
and dinner as well as any snacks (optional). Explain why your planned
diet is a healthy one.

4   Unscramble the letters to complete the sentence. Write the
whole sentence in your book.

A diet that contains
all the nutrients
the body needs
is a . . .

5   Prepare a recipe such as the **Pizza** below which has some of the foods
from the 'Eat Most' group, some from the 'Eat Moderately' group and
a little or none from the 'Eat Least' group.

Recipe to Try

Pizza

Ingredients

150 g S.R. flour (white or wholemeal)
1 tbsp oil
90 ml milk (approximately)
2 tbsp tomato purée
½ grated onion or 2 spring onions
100 g bacon pieces
¼ green pepper
100 g Cheddar cheese

Method

1   Grease a baking tray with a tiny amount of
oil.
2   Sift flour. Mix to a soft dough with the oil
and the milk
3   Roll the dough into a round and place on
baking tray.

4   Spread tomato purée on dough.
5   Top with onion, bacon, green pepper and
finally the grated cheese.
6   Bake at 220°C mark 7 for 20–30 minutes or
until golden.

Questions about the recipe

a   From which country does this recipe come?
b   How many parts of the Healthy Diet
Pyramid on page 44 are represented by the
ingredients in this recipe?
c   What other ingredients could be used on a
pizza?

Keeping Healthy

As a result of the health problems in Britain related to food, guidelines have been suggested that we should follow to become healthier people.

1 Eat a variety of foods each day.

2 Prevent and control obesity. Being too fat is a health hazard.

MILK
LENTILS

3 Eat less fat and have a healthier heart.

OIL
CREAM
CHIPS

SOFT DRINK
CHOCO

4 Eat less sugar.

5 Limit alcohol intake.

CRASH!
POOR DIET
SICKNESS

can all be caused by alcohol.

Can you find alcohol on the Healthy Diet Pyramid?

6 Eat more fruit and vegetables.

7 Eat less salt.

Each day you should have no more than 200 mg of salt.

= 750 mg salt

= 800 mg salt

CHIPS

= 300 mg salt

8 Drink more water.

9 Breast-feed babies.

Breast milk contains all the nutrients babies need for the first few months of life.

$1 + 2 + 3 + 4 + 5 + 6 + 7 + 8 + 9 =$

Healthier . . . ns

Workshop

1 As a class discuss the 9 guidelines for healthier Britons. Think of the ways that you can put these guidelines into practice.

2 Design a poster that would encourage pupils in your school to eat fruit and vegetables for snacks.

3 Conduct a fruit survey. Find out how much fruit each class member eats each day. Discuss ways in which you could include more fruit in your diet.

4 How much water do you drink? Keep a daily record chart for a week. How do you rate? Compare this with other members in your class.

5 Have a Water Week, when the whole class makes an effort to drink more water. Keep a daily record sheet and evaluate your findings.

6 Look at the foods available in your canteen. Divide them into good snack foods and poor snack foods. Give reasons for the way you divided them.

7 Plan three different snacks that would help to put into practice some of the 9 guidelines for healthier eating.

8 Make your own flavoured soft drink. Squeeze or extract 75 ml fresh fruit juice, pour into a glass over an ice cube and fill glass with water.

Practical Exercise No. 9
Healthy Cooking

Aim
- To experience sugar free and salt free cooking

Procedure
a Prepare the following recipes:

Recipe 1 Mashed Carrot

Ingredients

1 carrot
¼ tsp salt
250 ml water

Method

1 Wash and peel carrot. Cut into about
   6 pieces.
2 Place all ingredients into a saucepan and
   simmer for 15 minutes.
3 Drain water and mash with a fork.

Recipe 2 Mashed Carrot

Ingredients

1 carrot
250 ml water

Method

1 Wash and peel carrot. Cut into about
   6 pieces.
2 Place carrot and water into saucepan and
   simmer for 15 minutes.
3 Drain water and mash with a fork.

Recipe 3 Stewed fruit

Ingredients

1 piece ripe fruit
1 tbsp sugar
70 ml water

Method

1 Wash, peel, core and slice fruit if
   necessary.
2 Put all ingredients into a saucepan and
   simmer until fruit is tender.

Recipe 4 Stewed fruit

Ingredients

1 piece ripe fruit
70 ml water

Method

1 Wash, peel, core and slice fruit if
   necessary.
2 Put fruit and water in saucepan and
   simmer until fruit is tender.

b Taste each recipe.
c Draw up a table like the one below and record your findings.

Recipe	Appearance		Flavour		Reasons
	Good	Poor	Good	Poor	
1 Mashed Carrot						

d   If you rated Recipe 2 and 4 close to *poor* for flavour, try the following recipes:

Glazed Carrot

Ingredients

1 carrot
250 ml water
2 tbsp orange juice
a pinch of nutmeg

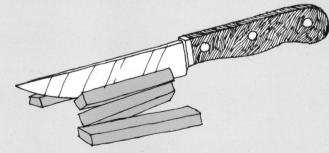

Method

1   Wash and peel carrot. Cut into sticks about the size of potato chips.
2   Place in saucepan with water. Simmer for 10 minutes.
3   Drain water from carrots. Add juice and simmer for 5 more minutes, allowing the juice to almost evaporate.
4   Sprinkle with nutmeg and serve.

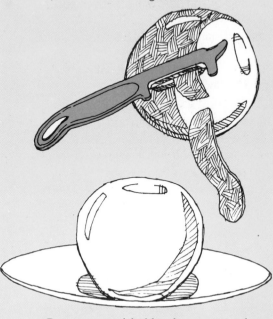

Spiked Apple

Ingredients

1 ripe cooking apple
70 ml water
1 pinch ground cloves or ground mixed spice
¼ tsp grated lemon rind

Method

1   Wash, core and slice apple.
2   Put all ingredients into saucepan and simmer until apple is 'glassy' in appearance.
3   Serve.

e   Draw up a table like the one you have done for Recipes 1 to 4, and record your findings.

Sugar Free Recipes to Try

Currant Delight

Pastry Ingredients

225 g wholemeal plain flour
150 g rolled oats
50g coconut
125 ml oil
250 ml water

Method

1 Mix flour, oats and coconut.
2 Beat oil and water together and add to dry ingredients.
3 Press into a greased Swiss roll tin.
4 Bake at 200°C mark 6 for 20–30 minutes.

Topping Ingredients

2 tsp lemon juice
250 g currants
300 ml water
3 tsp arrowroot
3 tsp water
1 tbsp coconut
2 tbsp sunflower seeds

Method

1 Combine currants, the 300 ml water and lemon juice.
2 Bring to the boil and simmer until soft.
3 Blend arrowroot and the 3 tsp water. Add to currants and stir until thickened.
4 Spread fruit mixture on cooked pastry and sprinkle with coconut and sunflower seeds.
5 Place in refrigerator to set.
6 Cut into squares.

Chinese Chews

Ingredients

110 g margarine
10 dates
100 ml water
125 g raisins
100 g dates (extra)
150 g wholemeal S.R. flour
1 egg
100 g walnuts
1 tsp vanilla essence

Method

1 Arrange oven shelf in centre of oven.
2 Set oven at 160°C mark 3.
3 Grease a slab tin, 18cm x 28cm (7″ x 11″).
4 Cut the 10 dates up roughly. Place in saucepan with the water. Bring to the boil and simmer for 10 minutes. Remove from cooker and beat with a wooden spoon until smooth.
5 Add margarine to hot date mixture and allow it to melt, mix well.
6 Cut raisins and the extra dates and walnuts into small pieces.
7 Beat egg slightly.
8 Add date mixture and egg to flour. Mix well.
9 Add fruits and vanilla and mix thoroughly.
10 Spread evenly into greased tin.
11 Bake for 25-30 minutes.
12 When cool, cut into finger lengths.

7 Exploring Food

In the last chapter you were introduced to a number of ways to select food for your daily diet. In this book we will be mainly using the Healthy Diet Pyramid as our guide. We will look at the pyramid layer by layer.

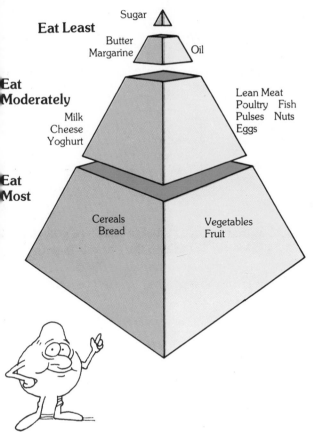

The Healthy Diet Pyramid

'Eat Most' Foods

These foods are essential for a healthy person. It is important for you to use these foods as a basis for your everyday diet, because:

- they are the best way to get the **energy** you need for all body functions.
- they keep your body **healthy**.

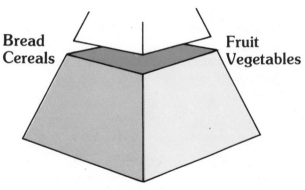

Whenever possible you should select **wholegrain** cereal products and **fresh** fruits and vegetables.

Cereals

Cereals are the seeds of grass plants that we can eat. These seeds are called grains. Some cereal grains that you may know are wheat, oats, rice, barley, rye and corn (maize).

If you cut a cereal grain in half and put it under a microscope it would look like this:

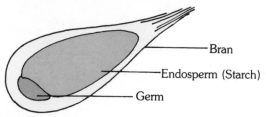

Bran
Endosperm (Starch)
Germ

The grain has three main parts:

Bran which gives us fibre to help food move through the body.

Endosperm which gives us starch for energy, and also contains protein.

Germ which contains the many nutrients needed for a new plant to start if the seed is planted.

Rarely do we eat the grains of cereals just as they come from the fields. In nearly all cases, they are prepared in some way in a mill or a factory.

These prepared cereals can contain the whole grain or different parts of the grain.

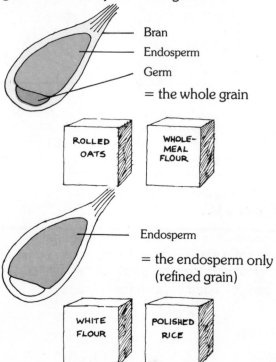

Bran
Endosperm
Germ
= the whole grain

ROLLED OATS   WHOLE-MEAL FLOUR

Endosperm
= the endosperm only (refined grain)

WHITE FLOUR   POLISHED RICE

Sometimes the refined products have extra nutrients added. They are then called **enriched** products.

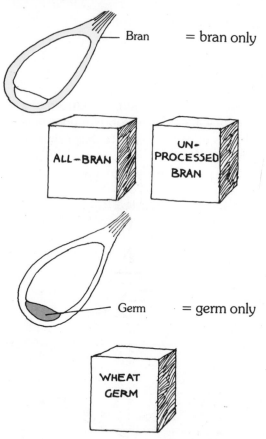

Bran   = bran only

ALL-BRAN   UN-PROCESSED BRAN

Germ   = germ only

WHEAT GERM

List as many more cereal products as you can for each type — look on the packets in your home or in the supermarket for help.

Flour is the most commonly used cereal product.

- How many different kinds of flour can you name?

- What do we use flour for?

As well as home baking, flour is used to make bread and pasta (the spaghetti family), which are both eaten all over the world.

Workshop

1 Complete the following definitions in your book.
A **wholegrain** cereal product is made from . . .
A **refined** cereal product is made from . . .
An **enriched** cereal product is made from . . .
cereal but with . . . added.

2 Draw a map of Britain in your book. On the map mark in areas where cereals are grown. This information can be found in your library or in your own atlas.

3 Complete this sentence in your book.
In Britain the largest cereal crop is . . .

4 The letters of each of the following words have been jumbled. Rearrange them to form the name of a cereal or cereal product. Write them in your book.

a OSTA
b WTEHA
c YER
d NROC
e RUOLF
f ICER
g DRAEB
h OLELRDAOTS
i RNCOROULF
j ASTPA
k YELBAR
l BNAR
m IMZEA
n SEKALFNRCO
o ALEMUROFLEOHWL

5 Identify the 6 cereals or cereal products in the list below. Write them in your book and say whether each is a cereal or a cereal product.
- bread
- tomato juice
- spaghetti
- olives
- salami
- cornflakes
- brown rice
- cheese
- muesli
- yoghurt
- cornflour
- beans

6 Cereal products are often consumed for breakfast. Conduct a survey to find out which cereals are commonly eaten for breakfast by members of your class (look back at p. 20 for notes on surveys if necessary). Compile your results. Which are the three most commonly eaten breakfast cereals in your class? Can you think of any reasons for this?

7 Prepare a recipe from the end of this workshop. What were the cereals in your recipe?

Practical Exercise No. 10
Cereals, Heat and Moisture

Aim
- To observe the reaction of a cereal to heat and moisture

Procedure

a Collect 2 tbsp polished rice from your teacher.

b Place 1 tbsp on a plate, saucer or piece of paper and set aside.

c Half fill a small saucepan with water. Bring the water to the boil and add the second tablespoon of rice. Simmer for 12 minutes. (Work on some of the activities in this workshop while you are waiting.)

d Pour the cooked rice and water into a sieve over the sink. Spread the drained rice onto a plate, saucer or piece of paper.

e Compare the two samples of rice. Write **true** or **false** beside each of the following statements about the **cooked** rice in your book.
   — The colour of the grain changes ....
   — The size of the grain remains the same ....
   — The grain swells ....
   — The texture of the grain alters..
   — The rice grain swells and becomes soft ....

f Measure the cooked rice. What did it measure? How did your result compare with the rest of the class? What was the *average* increase in measurement for cooked rice in your class?

- How will this help you when you are cooking rice for a meal?

Recipes to Try

Chicken Bread Rolls

Ingredients

1 pkt chicken noodle soup mix
250 ml water
50 g margarine
300 g wholemeal S.R. flour
1 egg, beaten
1 tbsp sesame seeds

Method

1   Collect all ingredients.

2   Whisk together the chicken noodle soup mix, water and margarine. Simmer for 5 minutes, stirring occasionally.

3   Sift S.R. flour into a large bowl. Stir in cooked soup mixture.

4   Remove dough from bowl and place on a floured board. Knead until mixture becomes smooth and elastic.

5   Cut dough into 6 pieces and shape into small rolls. Place on a lightly greased baking tray. Brush with egg yolk and sprinkle with sesame seeds.

6   Bake in a preheated oven 230°C mark 8 for 12 minutes. Serve hot.

Frankfurters with Noodles

Ingredients

4 frankfurters
½ pkt chicken flavoured 2 minute noodles
25 g grated cheese
2 tsp chopped parsley
pinch mixed herbs

Method

1   Collect all ingredients.

2   Add frankfurters to a large pan of boiling water. Boil for 5 minutes. Remove from water and allow to cool.

3   Bring 125 ml of water to the boil. Add 2 minute noodles and half the contents of flavour sachet. Cook for 2 minutes. Remove from heat.

4   Drain cooked noodles. Combine in a large bowl with cheese, parsley and mixed herbs.

5   Carefully slice frankfurters down the centre but not completely through. This will form a pocket. Carefully fill with noodle mixture.

6   Place on a baking tray and bake in a preheated 180°C mark 4 oven for 10 minutes.

Serves 2.

Breads

Bread is often called 'the staff of life'. This is because it forms the main part of meals in many countries throughout the world, and has done so for thousands of years.

● Which of your meals consist mainly of bread?

Bread is made in many shapes and sizes, and from different kinds of flour: wheat, rye, mixtures of different flours and whole grains. Sometimes other ingredients are added, such as vegetables, milk, cheese, raisins, sultanas and seeds such as poppy and sesame.

Bread and Your Diet

Bread is a carbohydrate food that supplies the body with energy. It also contains useful amounts of protein. When selecting bread choose high fibre, wholegrain or wholemeal bread.

Remember, fibre is important because it helps the passage of food through your body.

Workshop

1 Bread is a staple food in Britain. Make a list of the different types of bread available. Taste bread made from different types of flours. Draw up a table to compare the appearance, flavour and texture of different breads.

2 Discuss how you know that the bread you are buying is fresh that day.

3 Discuss methods of storing bread.
   What is the best method of storing bread for your family?

4 The breads below are readily available in most cities in Britain. Unjumble the letters of the words on their right to find out in which country each bread originated. Write them in your book.

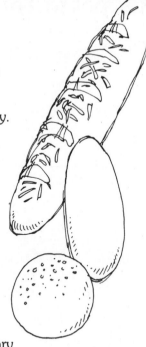

Baps.......................................CSOLNDTA
Tortillas.................................... OMEXIC
Poppadums....................................DNIIA
Pitta....................................... NLEABON
Pumpernickel...........................YGRENAM
Muffins .... GLNDAEN

5 Try a recipe or recipes from the end of this workshop. Use the glossary to look up any new Home Economics words.

Recipes to Try

Wholemeal Bread Rolls

Ingredients

250 g wholemeal flour
15 g fresh yeast or 3 teaspoons dried yeast
125 ml warm water
15 g sunflower margarine

Method

1 Crumble fresh yeast into warm water.

2 If using dried yeast, follow instructions on packet.

3 Rub margarine into flour.

4 Add enough water and yeast mixture to make an elastic dough.

5 Knead well on a floured surface.

6 Shape into 8 rolls.

7 Place on a greased baking tray, cover, and leave in a warm place for approximately 20 minutes, until risen. Remove cover.

8 Bake for 10 minutes in a hot oven 230°C mark 8.

Quick Pizza

Ingredients

1 thick slice wholemeal bread
½ tbsp tomato paste or one or two chopped tomatoes
pinch of mixed herbs
1 slice of salami or ham
small piece of green pepper
1 slice mozzarella cheese
or 50 g cheddar cheese (grated)

Method

1 Collect ingredients.

2 Using a knife spread the bread with the tomato paste.

3 Sprinkle the herbs over the tomato paste.

4 Top with remaining ingredients, finishing with the cheese.

5 Place on a baking tray and bake for 15-20 minutes in a preheated oven at 180°C mark 4.

6 Serve immediately.

Note: Other ingredients such as sardines, pineapple, anchovies, or leftover meat sauce may be used as topping.

Cheese and Herb Bread

Ingredients

250 g wholemeal flour
15 g fresh yeast or 3 teaspoons dried yeast
125 ml warm water
15 g sunflower margarine
25 g finely grated low-fat cheese
pinch mixed herbs

Method

1 Crumble fresh yeast into warm water.

2 If using dried yeast, follow instructions on packet.

3 Rub margarine into flour.

4 Add enough water and yeast mixture to make an elastic dough.

5 Knead dough on a floured surface until smooth, roll out into an oblong about 30 cm × 20 cm

6 Sprinkle the herbs and grated cheese over the dough, roll up and knead briefly.

7 Shape into a loaf and place in a well greased small loaf tin.

8 Cover and leave in a warm place to rise for 20 minutes.

9 When risen bake for 25–30 minutes at 220°C mark 7.

Fruits

Fruits are an important part of your daily diet.

- They supply **fibre** necessary for the passage of food through your body.

- They are a rich source of **vitamins** and **minerals**.

- They contain natural sugar called **fructose** which gives you energy.

- They supply a lot of **water** for body fluids, such as blood.

- Fruits add **variety** to your diets. They are colourful and give lots of pleasing flavours.

Ways of Buying Fruits

- **Fresh**
Fruit that is in season is fresh, full of flavour and cheap.

- **Canned**
Many canned fruits are available, giving us a wide choice of fruits all year round. It is best to buy fruits that have been canned in natural fruit juice or water to keep your sugar intake down.

- **Juice**
Fruit juice is a better choice than soft drinks which often contain lots of sugar. Buy fruit juices that do not have sugar added, or squeeze your own.

- **Dried Fruits**
Sultanas, raisins, currants, apples, apricots, pears, figs, dates.

- **Glacé Fruits**
Preserved in very thick sugar syrup.

- **Crystallised Fruits**
Preserved in sugar syrup and more sugar is added.

- **Frozen**

- Which types of fruits would be best to eat daily? Remember the guidelines for healthy living.

Fruit can be used in many ways in your diet.

- As a drink
- In bread
- In cakes
- As snacks
- As a first course or entree
- In yoghurt
- In biscuits
- As a sauce, e.g. apple sauce with roast pork
- In a dessert
- In a salad
- With the main course, e.g. pineapple with ham; lamb with apricots

Workshop

1 Fruits are often classified, that is divided into groups, according to the way they grow or the way they look. Below are examples of grouping (classifying) fruits. Hidden in the jumbled letters are examples of fruits that belong to each group. Make a list of each group of fruits in your book by unscrambling the letters.
Can you add more fruits to each list?

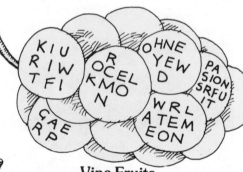

Citrus Fruits

These fruits have a skin that can be easily removed. They grow on trees with shiny, green leaves.

Seed Fruits

These fruits have tiny seeds in the centre. They grow on trees.

Stone Fruits

These fruits have large stones in the centre and grow on trees.

Vine Fruits

These fruits grow on vines.

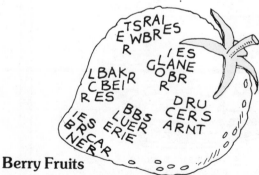

Berry Fruits

These fruits grow on small plants, shrubs or vines. They are small and have similar keeping qualities.

Sub-tropical and Tropical Fruits

These fruits grow in tropical climates.

Recipes to Try

Frozen Fruit Sherbet

Ingredients

2-3 pieces of fruit of your own choice
juice of 1 orange
1 eggwhite

Method

1 ·Mash pieces of fruit together with a fork or other suitable utensil.
2 Mix the fruit with the orange juice.
3 Beat the eggwhite until stiff.
4 Add the white into the fruit mixture.
5 Place in a dish and put in the freezer until frozen.
6 Serve in a dish or a cone.
7 Decorate with chopped nuts or a glacé cherry.

Apple Crumble

Ingredients

100 g wholemeal flour
or 50 g wholemeal flour
    50 g plain flour
25 g raw cane sugar
50 g sunflower margarine

500 g cooking apples
50 g dried fruit
½ teaspoon mixed spice

Method

1 Wash, peel, core and slice apples.
2 Put apples into a saucepan, add dried fruit, spice and 2 tablespoons water. Bring to the boil, simmer for 5 minutes.
3 Put cooked fruit into an ovenproof dish.
4 Make crumble by rubbing fat into flour until mixture looks like breadcrumbs, stir in sugar.
5 Spoon crumb mixture over fruit in dish.
6 Bake in oven 190°C mark 5 for 20 minutes.

Serves 4.

Fruit Bars

Ingredients

60 g dried apricots
60 g dates
60 g raisins
30 g ground almonds (or other ground nuts)
30-60 g coconut .

Method

1 Put all the dried fruit through a fine mincer.
2 Place fruit and almonds into a bowl and work together with enough coconut to make a firm mouldable mixture.
3 Roll in extra coconut and form into 'logs' about 1½ cm x 8 cm. Wrap in cling film and refrigerate until firm.

Fruit salad

Ingredients

1 red skinned apple
1 orange
1 banana

syrup:
    250 ml water
    25 g raw cane sugar
    1 lemon

or in place of
syrup use 250 ml
pure fruit juice

Method

1 Put 250 ml water into saucepan, add sugar.
2 Heat until sugar is dissolved. Leave to cool. Add lemon juice.
3 Put syrup or fruit juice into serving dish.
4 Skin the orange and banana. Wash the apple. Cut the fruit into small pieces, placing in syrup immediately to prevent browning.

Other fruits may be added if available in summer: cherries, strawberries, raspberries, peaches, kiwi fruit.

Serves 3.

Pineapple Hats

Ingredients

4 slices of pineapple
4 apricot halves
1 glacé cherry
a little whipped cream (one 250 ml carton for
the whole class)

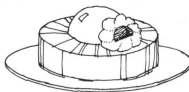

Method

1 Place each slice of pineapple in a serving
   dish (flat glass dishes look the best).
2 Place an apricot half neatly over the hole
   in the centre of the pineapple (curved
   side upwards).
3 Cut the cherry into 4 pieces.
4 Pipe a star of cream at the 'brim' of the hat
   and add a cherry 'jewel'.

Fruit Flan

Ingredients

50 g wholemeal flour
50 g raw cane sugar
2 eggs
fresh or tinned fruit

Method

1 Break eggs into mixing bowl, add sugar.
2 Whisk with rotary or electric whisk until
   mixture is very thick.
3 Fold flour into whisked mixture.
4 Pour mixture into a greased 18cm flan tin.
5 Bake at 190°C gas mark 5 until risen and
   spongy, approximately 20 minutes.
6 Turn out flan onto cooling tray. Allow to
   cool.
7 Fill with fresh or tinned fruit.
8 A glaze can be made by blending 2 tsps of
   arrowroot with 125 ml of fruit juice: bring to
   the boil, allow to cool slightly and pour over
   fruit in flan.

Serves 4–6.

Vegetables

Vegetables are important in your diet. They
provide:
- vitamins
- minerals
- fibre
- water
- energy
- colour and texture

Three servings of vegetables a day are part of a
healthy diet.

Buying Vegetables

It is a good idea to buy vegetables when they
are in season. This is when they are cheapest
and best.
Sometimes it is difficult to do this. Many
methods of keeping (preserving) vegetables
have been developed to enable us to have
most vegetables all year round.

Fresh

Canned

Frozen

Dehydrated or Dried

Cooking Vegetables

Vegetables add variety and colour to your meals. There are many ways of preparing them. The only limitation is your imagination.

Stir Fried

Boiled

Fried

Fresh
in salads

Grilled

Baked

In Cakes and Breads

Pressure-cooked

Workshop

1 **Class Quiz** *How many vegetables can you think of?*
   - Divide the class in two.
   - The teacher will act as the scorer.
   - Each side is to name a vegetable.
   - A recorder keeps a list of each vegetable named for each group.
   - If a vegetable is repeated the team loses a point. The game ends when neither side can name another vegetable. The side that can name the most vegetables wins.
   - Did this game help you to realise just how many vegetables there are?

2 **Canned Vegetables**
   Visit a supermarket or local shop.
   a Take note of how many types of vegetables are canned.
   b Carefully read the labels on the vegetable cans. Note how many vegetables have added sugar and salt in them.
   - Discuss why the vegetables have added sugar and salt in them.
   - How might this information help you in your choice of vegetables? Remember it is wise to keep your sugar and salt intake low.

YOU DECIDE!

3 **Cooking Vegetables**

The same vegetable can be cooked in many different ways. Find and write in your book as many ways as you can that potatoes can be prepared and served.

● Discuss this as a class and compare your results.

4 Unscramble the letters in the following words. They will give you the names of different vegetables. Write the names of the vegetables in your book.

a TUTLEEC

b ABBAGEC

c CLERYE

d ROBUSTSANEP

e GRPAAASUS

f SANEB

g ASPE

h OTSTAPOE

i SOINON

j AORTCRS

k MRORWA

l COCBROLI

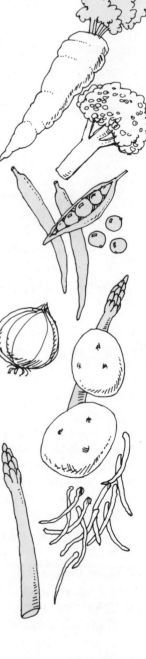

5 **Classes of Vegetables**

Vegetables can be classified into groups according to the part of the plant we eat.

Copy the list below into your book. Place the vegetables you have found in Activity 4 alongside the group you think they belong to.

Class

Shoots...

Stalks...

Leaves...

Flowers...

Seeds ....

Fruit...

Bulbs...

Tubers...

Roots...

● Discuss your answers with your class. How many did you have correct?

6 Try some of the vegetable recipes at the end of this workshop.

Recipes to Try

Vegetable Soup

Ingredients

⅓ carrot
¼ onion
1 stick celery
⅓ parsnip
2 sprigs parsley
1 stock cube
500 ml water
25 g rice

Method

1   Wash and peel vegetables.
2   Grate onion and parsnip.
3   Cut carrot and celery into 1 cm cubes.
4   Crumble stock cube into water and place all ingredients except parsley into a saucepan. Bring to the boil.
5   Simmer the soup for 30 minutes with the lid on.
6   Chop parsley finely and sprinkle over the soup.

Serves 2.

Questions about the recipe

a   Why does the body need vegetables?

b   How many servings of vegetables should you have each day?

c   To cut food into cubes is to . . .
   ● slice
   ● dice
   ● cut
   ● shred

d   A vegetable can be cut up safely . . .
   ● held in the hand
   ● in a bowl
   ● on the bench
   ● on a wooden chopping board

e   To check the contents of a hot saucepan, you should . . .
   ● bend over the pot
   ● lift the lid of the pot away from you
   ● lift the lid of the pot towards you
   ● remove the saucepan to the bench

f   Explain the difference between *boiling* and *simmering*.

g   When do you usually have soup?
   ● For breakfast
   ● At the start of a meal
   ● At the end of a meal

Tomato Soup

Ingredients

1 large tin tomatoes
1 rasher bacon
1 onion
1 medium sized potato
pinch herbs
salt and pepper
1 tablespoon sunflower oil
125 ml skimmed milk

Method

1   Chop onion and bacon, fry together in oil for about 5 minutes.
2   Add diced potato, tomatoes and juice and 125 ml water.
3   Add seasonings.
4   Simmer gently until potato is soft for approximately 30 minutes.
5   Blend in liquidiser until smooth.
6   Return to saucepan, add milk, reheat.

Serves 2.

Stir Fried Vegetables

Ingredients

50 g green beans
50 g mushrooms
1 spring onion
small piece red pepper
1 tomato
1 stick of celery
50 g sweetcorn
100 g fresh bean sprouts
2 tsps oil
1 tsp soy sauce

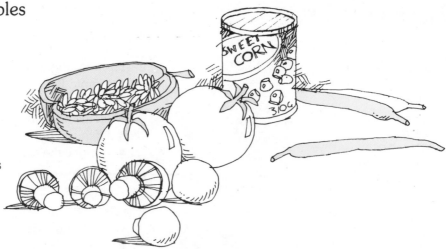

Method

1 Collect all ingredients.
2 Slice beans, mushrooms, spring onions, red capsicum, tomatoes and celery.
3 Wash and drain bean shoots.
4 Heat oil in a large frying pan or wok.
5 Stir in prepared vegetables and allow to cook for 5 minutes, stirring gently.
6 Add soy sauce before serving.

Serves 2–3.

Vegetables in Cheese Sauce

Ingredients

250 ml skimmed milk
15 g cornflour
pinch of salt and pepper
100 g low fat cheddar cheese
1 small cauliflower (broken into florets)
or 4 medium sized leeks (washed and cut into rings), or, a mixture of vegetables eg 1 potato (peeled and cut into 2 cm cubes), 1 carrot (peeled and cut into ½ cm slices), and 3 or 4 cauliflower florets

Method

1 Cook vegetables in boiling water: cauliflower 10 minutes, leeks 15 minutes, carrots 20 minutes, potatoes 20 minutes.
2 Make sauce by blending cornflour and a little milk in a saucepan, then add the remaining milk.
3 Bring to the boil, stirring continuously, until sauce boils and thickens.
4 Remove from heat and stir in salt, pepper and grated cheese. Save one tablespoon cheese.
5 Place the cooked vegetables in an ovenproof dish and pour the cheese sauce over.
6 Sprinkle with the remaining cheese and brown under a hot grill.

Serves 3.

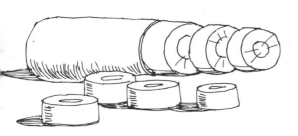

Jacket Potato

Ingredients

1 potato
1 tsp butter (optional)
1 sprig parsley

Method

1   Scrub potato until quite clean.

2   Prick with a fork.

3   Place straight onto oven shelf.

4   Bake at oven temperature of 190°C for about 1 hour or until a skewer will pass through the thickest part of the potato.

5   Cut a cross on the top and garnish with butter and parsley.

Serves 1.

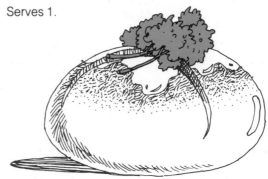

Carrot Rings

Ingredients

300 g carrots
¼ tsp salt (optional)

Method

1   Peel carrots and cut into ½ cm slices.

2   Place about 3 cm water into a saucepan with salt and bring to the boil.

3   Add carrots. Cover and boil for 15 minutes or until tender.

Serves 4.

Minted Peas

Ingredients

500 g peas
a little mint
pinch of salt (optional)
1 tsp butter (optional)

Method

1   Shell peas.

2   Boil water, salt and mint.

3   Add peas. Cover and boil for 10-15 minutes, or until tender.

4   Drain and toss in butter if wished.

Serves 4.

'Eat Moderately' Foods

It is recommended that you have two servings from this group each day. Children should consume 600 ml of milk daily, or an equivalent amount of cheese. (30–40 g of cheese is equal to 200 ml of milk.)

'Eat Moderately' Foods are essential for growth and repair of your body tissue and for general good health.

The Healthy Diet Pyramid

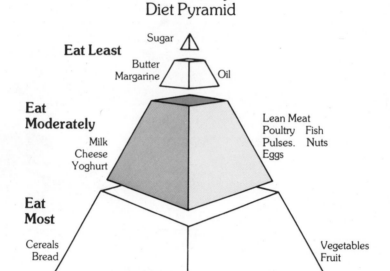

Eat Least — Sugar

Butter
Margarine — Oil

Eat Moderately

Milk
Cheese
Yoghurt

Lean Meat
Poultry   Fish
Pulses.   Nuts
Eggs

Eat Most

Cereals
Bread

Vegetables
Fruit

Dairy Foods

Dairy foods include milk and all milk products.

Milk and You

Milk is the first food of mammals. It contains all the food that the new born mammal may need, from birth until it is several months old. At your age milk is especially important for the growth of healthy bones and teeth.

Milk is available in many forms

Pasteurised milk is heated to a high temperature to kill most of the bacteria, then cooled quickly. This stops diseases from spreading.

Bottled Milk (Pasteurised)

As well as being pasteurised, carton milk is homogenised. This stops the cream from rising to the top of the milk.

Carton Milk (Homogenised and Pasteurised)

Some of the water is removed from the milk.

Evaporated Milk

Milk is sprayed onto hot rollers and all the water is removed by evaporation.

Powdered or Dried Milk

Some of the water in the milk is removed and cane sugar is added.

Condensed Milk

Heat-treated to keep for a long time unopened.

There are also many 'special' milks that come in cartons.

High Protein Low Fat Milk   **Flavoured Milk**   **Skimmed Milk (fat removed)**

Skimmed Milk has the fat (cream) removed. It is called 'skimmed' because in the past the cream was skimmed off the top of the milk by hand.

Research

Find out how milk gets from the farm to you.

Workshop

1   Draw a map of Britain in your book. Find out the major areas of dairy farming in Britain. Shade and name the areas on your map. How close do you live to a dairy farming area?
   • How do the people who do not live near dairy farms get fresh milk daily?

2   In the picture of the cow below are the letters to make up 8 products that come from the cow. Can you find them? Write the answers in your book. Use each letter only once.

3   Milk is used in many ways in cooking. In the puzzle below, find 10 ways that milk can be used in cooking. List the words in your book as you find them.

```
S A U C E S U M S
O Y J U N K E T C
U B I S C U I T O
P A S T A T A T N
S I C A K E S A E
N J O R B R E A D
P L E Q U I C H E
Q M S D R I N K S
```

4 Correct storage of dairy products is important.
   Discuss how you would store the following items: a carton of milk, an
   unopened packet of cheddar cheese, a packet of cheese slices, a carton
   of long-life (UHT) milk, a piece of cheese, a carton of yoghurt.
   Write the storage methods and reasons for each method in your book.

5 There are hundreds of different types of cheeses available in Britain.
   Rearrange the letters of the words below to find the names of 12
   famous cheeses. You can help each other with this exercise.

   a EBRI   g LUEBVNIE
   b CDAEHDR   h YNWELSEEADL
   c NTOLTSI   i PMESARAN
   d OETATGC   j AZLEAORZLM
   e EEHCHIRS   k ADOUG
   f MDEA   l AMECMTBER

6 Milk comes in many forms to meet the needs of people. Read the
   following stories and decide which is the wisest choice of milk for each.
   Give reasons for your choice.

   a Sally is going hiking. She can only carry 15 kg including her
      sleeping bag. It is not necessary to carry water as the party will
      follow the river. What type of milk should Sally take?

   b Joe's family does not drink a lot of fresh milk. They do not use milk
      in tea or coffee, and use powdered milk for cooking. Joe's mother
      does not like to give visitors powdered milk. What type of milk
      could the family purchase to ensure that they have milk on hand
      when visitors call?

7 Yoghurt can form the basis of many snacks or desserts. Here is an
   example.

Yoghurt Banana Split

Method

1 Peel and slice a ripe banana in half.

2 Spoon over some yoghurt.

3 Top with chopped walnuts and serve.

Make up your own yoghurt snack. You can
use all sorts of fruits, nuts and toppings.
Give your recipe a name and write out your
recipe using the following headings:

ingredients, method, no. of servings. In fact
your class could make their own book of
yoghurt recipes.

Practical Exercise No. 11
Cheese Tasting

Aim
- To describe and taste 6 different types of cheese

Procedure

a   Draw up a taste chart as set out below in your book.

Type of cheese	Colour	Flavour	Your rating

b   Your teacher will arrange on plates the 6 different cheeses for tasting.

c   Mild cheeses will be tasted first.

d   Look carefully at the cheeses. Note the colour of each cheese on your taste chart. These words may help you to describe the colour: white, pale, clear, yellow, dark, light, cream, ivory, orange, blue, blue/green, metal.

e   Describe the flavour or taste of the cheese.

We taste food with our tongue. There are about 9000 taste buds on the tongue which identify **four** main tastes: sweet, bitter, sour, and salty. All other tastes are a mixture of these four.

Four different areas of the tongue respond to the four main tastes. Example:

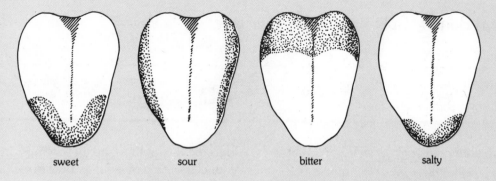

sweet   sour   bitter   salty

Some of the words you could use to describe flavour are: bitter, sweet, salty, sharp, peppery, delicate, fresh, strong, biting, mild, nutty.

YOU DECIDE!

f   Rate each cheese according to how much you liked or disliked it. To do this you can give points as below:

Dislike a lot... 1 point
Dislike... 2 points
Neither like nor dislike .... 3 points
Like .... 4 points
Like a lot .... 5 points

For example, if you like the cheese a lot you will give it 5 points, if you dislike it you will give it 2, and so on. Total the answers for the whole class on the board. The cheese with the highest score is the most popular cheese.

g   When you have completed the exercise answer these questions:

— Which is the most *popular* cheese with the class?

— Which cheese is the most *unpopular*?

●   Discuss the possible reasons for these results.

Research
Find out how cheese is made.

Recipes to Try

Cheese and Potato Pie

Ingredients

500 g potatoes
100 g low fat cheddar cheese
2 tablespoons skimmed milk
pepper

Method

1   Peel, wash and cut potatoes into even-sized pieces then cook for 20 minutes until soft.
2   When potatoes are cooked, drain and mash with milk and two-thirds of the grated cheese.
3   Put into serving dish.
4   Sprinkle on the rest of the cheese.
5   Brown under a hot grill.
6   Garnish with tomato and parsley.
Serves 2.

Custard

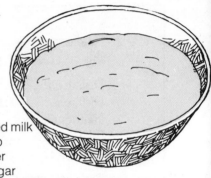

Ingredients

250 ml skimmed milk
1 rounded tbsp
custard powder
1 level tbsp sugar

Method

1   Place custard powder in small bowl and blend with a little milk.
2   Place blended custard powder and all other ingredients into a small saucepan on medium to low heat.
3   Stir mixture *constantly* until it thickens.
4   Remove from heat and serve.
Serves 2–3.

Scalloped Potatoes

Ingredients

350 g potatoes
pinch salt and pepper
1 tbsp flour
250 ml milk
1 tbsp margarine

Method

1   Peel, wash and cut potatoes into thin slices.
2   Place potatoes in casserole, sprinkling each layer with flour, salt, pepper and small pieces of margarine.
3   Heat milk, pour over potato and cover.
4   Bake for about 50-60 minutes at 190°C. mark 5.
Serves 4.

Meat

In Britain the main sources of meat are sheep, cattle, pigs and poultry (mainly chicken). Meat from these animals provides an important source of protein, fat, minerals and vitamins.

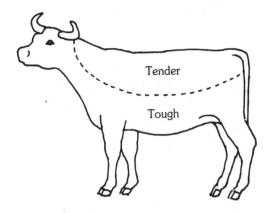

Tender

Tough

- Discuss the ways in which meat is included in your diet.
- What is your favourite meat? Why?
- What type of meat or meat dishes would you be most likely to buy from the takeaway food shop?

We eat a lot of meat in Britain.
Each person eats an average of 150 g of meat daily. Remember that when working out averages for a population, everyone is counted, including babies and vegetarians.
Ask your teacher to weigh 150 g of meat for you to look at. Do you eat that much meat daily?
Think about this average daily amount.

- As meat is an 'eat moderately' food, do we eat too much, too little or just enough meat?

Meat can be broadly classified as being tough or tender. Whether it is tough or tender affects the method we select for cooking the meat.

Tough Meats
These come from parts of the animal that are well exercised, like the neck and legs, and usually require longer periods of cooking than other cuts of meat. Suitable methods for cooking tough meats include baking, roasting, stewing, braising and as a casserole.

Tender Meats
These come from parts of the animal that do not get a lot of movement, so the muscles are not as well developed. These cuts do not need to be cooked for a long time, so quicker methods of cooking like grilling, frying and barbecueing can be used.

As there are more of the tougher cuts of meat on an animal than tender cuts, the tender cuts are usually more expensive.

- Which type of meat adds the most to the fuel bill for cooking — tough or tender?

Meats can also be used to make a wide variety of sausages and meat loaves.

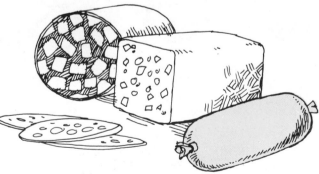

- Discuss the ways that meat changes when it is cooked. (Look at samples if possible.)
- Make a list of these changes in your book or on the board.
- Why is it usual for us to cook meat?

Workshop

1 Either invite a local butcher to your class to talk about meat and show you how a carcass is cut up, or your class could arrange to visit the local butchers shop for the same purpose.

2 Copy the chart below into your book.

Cattle	Sheep	Pig	Poultry

Where do the meats listed below come from? Put each meat or meat cut under the correct source in the chart.

pork, veal, steak, lamb, turkey, bacon, ham, mutton (very little eaten in Britain), beef, chicken, drumstick, duck

3 Match the different methods of cooking meat with their correct definitions. Write them in your book.

Grilling   Roasting   Frying   Stewing   Casserole

- Cooking a small or a large amount of food in oil
- Cooking in the dry heat of an oven
- Quick method of cooking under direct heat
- Moist method of cooking meat in an enclosed container on the top of the stove
- Long slow method of cooking in a container in the oven

Recipes to Try

Golden Chicken Casserole

Ingredients

2 chicken portions
1 rasher lean bacon
1 onion
1 chicken stock cube
small tin sweetcorn
pepper
1 rounded tbsp cornflour
1 tbsp vegetable oil

Method

1　Chop onion. Remove skin from chicken.
　Chop bacon.

2　Fry chicken, onion and bacon until chicken
　is browned on outside.

3　Transfer chicken, bacon and onion to
　casserole dish.

4　Dissolve stock cube in 250 ml boiling
　water.

5　Put stock in frying pan. Blend in cornflour,
　made to a smooth paste with 1 tablespoon
　cold water.

6　Bring to the boil, stirring well, until the
　mixture thickens.

7　Pour sauce over chicken. Stir in sweetcorn.
　Put lid on dish.

8　Bake in oven 180°C mark 4 for 1 hour.

Serves 2.

Questions about the recipe

a　Why is it healthier to remove the skin from
　the chicken?

b　Why should a casserole be cooked with the
　lid on?

Beefburgers

Ingredients

250 g lean minced beef
1 slice wholemeal bread
1 medium sized onion
1 egg
1 dessertspoon tomato ketchup
pepper

Method

1　Make breadcrumbs by rubbing bread
　through sieve or use a liquidiser.

2　Grate onion or chop finely, beat egg, or
　blend egg and onion in liquidiser.

3　Mix all ingredients together in mixing bowl

4　Shape into beefburgers. Makes 2 very
　large or 4 medium sized burgers.

5　Grill for 15 minutes each side. Cover grill
　pan grid with foil to make turning
　beefburgers easier.

6　Serve with toasted beefburger buns and
　salad.

Serves 2

Questions about the recipe

a　How many people does this recipe serve?

b　What other vegetables and fruit could you
　use in a hamburger?

c　What is the function of the egg in this
　recipe?

d　Work out the cost of your beefburgers.

Shepherd's Pie

Ingredients

250 g lean minced beef
1 onion
1 beef stock cube
100 g carrots
500 g potatoes
2 tbsp skimmed milk
pepper
25 g cornflour

Method

1. Peel, slice and finely chop the onion.
2. Dry fry minced beef and onion until meat is browned.
3. Pour away any excess fat.
4. Add diced carrot and stock cube dissolved in 250 ml boiling water. Leave to simmer.
5. Peel potatoes, cut into even-sized pieces, simmer for 20 minutes.
6. When potatoes are cooked, mash with pinch of pepper and skimmed milk.
7. Blend 1 tablespoon cornflour with 1 tablespoon cold water.
8. Add to meat mixture. Bring to boil, stirring all the time until the mixture thickens.
9. Put meat in dish.
10. Spread potato carefully on top.
11. Bake in oven 190°C mark 5 for 20 minutes until potato is browned on top.

Serves 2–3.

Chicken Tacos

Ingredients

100 g chicken meat
1 tbsp chives or 1 spring onion
½ tbsp oil
½ tsp chilli sauce (Chilli sauce is very hot — add more or less to suit your taste.)
1 taco shell
shredded lettuce
¼ tomato, chopped
sour cream or plain yoghurt
¼ green pepper

Method

1. Collect all ingredients.
2. Slice chicken into small pieces.
3. Wash pepper and chives and chop up finely.
4. Heat oil in a pan. Add chicken and cook for 5 minutes.
5. Stir in chives, green pepper and chilli sauce.
6. Heat taco shell as directed on the packet.
7. Spoon the mixture into the shell.
8. Top with shredded lettuce, chopped tomato and sour cream or yoghurt.
9. Serve immediately.

Serves 1.

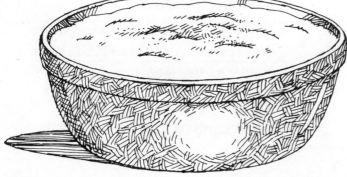

Spaghetti Bolognaise

Ingredients

250 g lean minced beef
1 medium sized cooking onion
1 small tin (142 g) tomato purée
1 teaspoon mixed herbs
pinch black pepper
1 beef stock cube
100 g mushrooms
100 g wholewheat spaghetti

Method

Bolognaise sauce

1　Peel, slice and finely chop the onion.
2　Fry chopped onion and beef. Do not add any fat.
3　When meat is brown, drain off any excess fat.
4　Add tomato purée and stock cube dissolved in 125 ml boiling water.
5　Add herbs and a pinch of black pepper.
6　Leave to simmer gently for 30 minutes.
7　Add washed and sliced mushrooms and simmer for 15 minutes longer.

Spaghetti

1　Half fill a medium sized saucepan with water.
2　Bring to the boil. Slowly fold in the spaghetti.
3　Stir gently until water returns to boil.
4　Boil for 12 minutes stirring occasionally.
5　Drain and serve topped with the sauce.

Serves 2–3.

Questions about the recipe

a　Which country did this recipe come from?
b　To which group of foods does spaghetti belong on the Healthy Diet Pyramid?
c　There are a lot of different shapes of spaghetti-type foods. They all come under one name. What is it?

Irish Stew

Ingredients

4 loin or chump lamb chops
250 ml water
3 shakes pepper
2 onions
500 g potatoes
1 tsp chopped parsley
1 beef stock cube

Method

1　Trim any excess fat from chops.
2　Slice onions.
3　Place all ingredients, except potatoes and parsley, into a saucepan and bring to the boil. Simmer for 20 minutes.
4　Peel and wash potatoes and cut into 1 cm thick slices.
5　Lift chops into a casserole.
6　Cover meat with neatly arranged layers of potatoes, then pour the liquid and onions over potato.
7　Put lid on casserole and place in oven on 200°C mark 6 for 40 minutes.
8　Garnish with chopped parsley.

Serves 4.

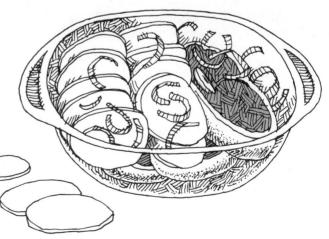

Eggs

Did you know?

Eggs have been a food item for over 5000 years.

Primitive man ate the eggs of wild birds.

The hens that lay most of the eggs we eat used to be wild birds.

Eggs contain: protein, fat, vitamins, minerals.

Eggs may be substituted for meat in the diet. Eggs that are sold through shops have all been graded according to their weight. For example a size 3 egg weighs 60–65 g. Most recipes are worked out for size 3 eggs. Sizes range from 1 to 7.

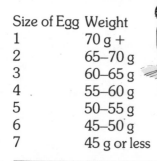

Size of Egg	Weight
1	70 g +
2	65–70 g
3	60–65 g
4	55–60 g
5	50–55 g
6	45–50 g
7	45 g or less

Eggs have many uses in cookery:

- lightening mixtures

Soufflé   Custard

Pavlova   Sponge cakes

- thickening foods as in custards
- enriching foods, as in cakes, pastry, and breads to give them extra nutrients
- holding foods together (binding) as in meatballs, fish cakes
- protecting foods during cooking, e.g. some foods are coated in egg and breadcrumbs before cooking. The egg helps to seal the food and keep the frying fat out.

Eggs are often used as a main course or part of a meal, for example, boiled eggs for breakfast. List as many main courses as you can think of that use eggs. You may be able to find two or three illustrations from magazines and recipe books to assist you.

Workshop

1   Although hen's eggs are the main eggs that we buy to eat, other eggs can be eaten. Solve the word puzzles in the eggs to find out which other eggs we might eat.

2   Answer **true** or **false** to each of the following statements.
   a   Eggs contain lots of protein.
   b   Protein is used by the body for growth and repair.
   c   Eggs are nutritious because they contain all the nutrients for the new chick.
   d   Most of the eggs we eat come from ducks.
   e   Eggs give us carbohydrate for energy.
   f   Eggs are a good source of vitamins.

3   Practical Exercise No. 13.

4   Practical Exercise No. 14.

Practical Exercise No. 13
Exploring Eggs

Aim
- To explore the structure of an egg

Procedure
a   Collect the following equipment:
   1 egg
   1 tea plate
   1 skewer
   1 medium sized bowl, half filled with water.

b   Ensure that all equipment is very clean so that you will be able to use the egg in a recipe.

c   Observe the shape of the egg. Sketch it in your book.

d   Carefully crack the egg and break the shell in half as evenly as possible. Carefully empty the egg from the shell onto the plate — don't break the yolk.

e   Examine the inside of the two pieces of shell. Handle them very carefully, you need them whole. Are they the same? You should have one half that has a bubble in it (the more rounded end), and one half that is quite smooth inside (the more pointed end). Find out (from your teacher) what the bubble is for.

f   You can see from the bubble that the shell has a layer of skin stuck to the inside. This skin is called the **membrane**. *Very carefully* peel the membrane from the shell with the bubble; you must handle it carefully so as not to crack the shell.

g   Now float both pieces of shell, i.e. the half with the membrane and the half without, in the bowl of water. Put the bowl aside.

h   Examine the egg on the plate.

i   Describe the egg white (the clear part).

j   Describe the egg yolk (the yellow part).
   Can you see a lightish spot on the yolk?
   Can you see a little white twisted cord on each side of the yolk?

k   Draw what you see in your book. Label your drawing; ask your teacher to help where necessary. Some eggs may be easier to observe than others; it depends on how gently they slip from the shell, and how fresh they are. (Ask your teacher to show you how you can tell whether a whole egg is fresh.)

l   Take your skewer and pierce the yolk once or twice. What happened? What did you break with the skewer (that is, what was holding the yolk in a round shape)? Add another label to your drawing.

m   Look at your floating egg shells. What has happened? (A result is usually obvious after 15 minutes of floating.) What have you learnt about the shell? What is the function of the shell membrane?

n   A whole egg looks like this in cross-section:

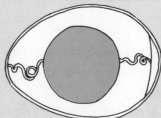

● From what you have learnt during this exercise, draw and label the above diagram in your book.

Practical Exercise No. 14
Separating and Whisking Eggs

Aim
To compare different methods of separating eggs and whisking egg whites

Procedure
Read through the whole exercise before beginning.

a   Each of you will need one egg and the following equipment:
1 mixing bowl
1 small basin
1 knife

b   Form groups of three, each pupil in the group to use a different method of separating eggs:
using the shells
using an egg separator
using a plate and egg cup

c   Put the yolk into a small basin. Put the white into a clean mixing bowl.

d   Working in groups again investigate different methods of whisking egg whites:

balloon whisk
rotary whisk
electric hand whisk

Using the different whisks, whisk the egg whites until they stand in peaks. Time how long this takes and record your results.

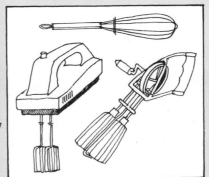

Discussion
As a class compare results and discuss the following questions.

Separating Eggs
Decide which is the
    quickest
    easiest
    safest
method of separating eggs.

Whisking Egg Whites
Which is the quickest method of whisking egg whites?

Which is the most labour-saving method of whisking egg whites?

Does the size of the mixing bowl used make any difference to the time taken to whisk?

If you broke yolks when separating eggs and then whisked the white with some yolk, did this affect the whisking?

Use the yolk and whisked white to make an Apple Amber. If you broke your yolk, add 25g flour to the recipe and make a small whisked sponge to use on top of the apples.

Recipes to Try

Apple Amber

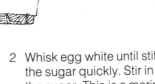

Ingredients

200 g cooked apple
2 tsps lemon juice
or ¼ tsp cinnamon
1 egg yolk
1 egg white
25 g sugar

Method

1   Beat egg yolk into cooked apple. Add lemon juice or cinnamon and place in a small ovenproof dish.

2   Whisk egg white until stiff, whisk in half of the sugar quickly. Stir in the other half of the sugar. This is a meringue mixture.

3   Pile meringue on top of apple, draw into peaks with the back of a tablespoon.

4   Bake for 20 minutes at 180°C mark 4 until meringue is a pale golden colour.

Serves 2.

Omelette

Ingredients

2 eggs
1 tbsp water
a dash of salt
a shake of pepper
1 tbsp oil

Equipment

1 frying pan or omelette pan
1 fork
a small mixing bowl
1 spatula
measuring spoons

Method

1 Lightly mix eggs, water, salt and pepper.
Don't beat!

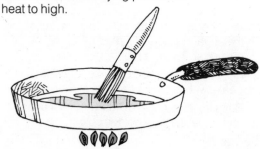

2 Warm your frying pan over low heat.

3 Brush oil on to hot frying pan. Turn
heat to high.

4 Pour eggs all at once into frying pan.
Do it quickly.

5 Tip pan as you go. Push cooked egg to
centre as the uncooked egg runs to the
edges and sets.

6 While centre is still runny flip the sides over
to the middle.

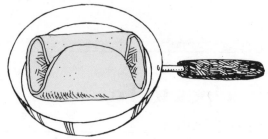

7 Turn out onto plate and serve immediately.

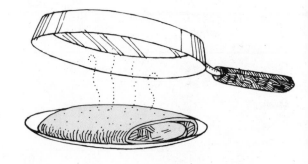

Bread and Butter Pudding

Ingredients

3 thick slices wholemeal bread
25 g margarine
25 g sugar
1 level tsp mixed spice
50 g dried fruit
2 eggs
500 ml skimmed milk

Method

1 Spread bread with the margarine and cut into fingers, small squares or triangles.
2 Beat eggs and mix with warmed milk (not hot).
3 Put half the bread in a greased 1 litre ovenproof dish. Sprinkle with half of the fruit, sugar and spice. Repeat, with remaining ingredients.
4 Pour eggs and milk over the bread mixture.
5 Place in oven 180°C mark 4 until set and crisp and browned on top.

Serves 4.

Baked Sweetcorn, Cheese and Rice

Ingredients

½ small onion, chopped
150 g sweetcorn
75 g grated cheese
150 g cooked rice
1 tsp sunflower margarine
2 eggs
1 stick chopped celery

Method

1 Fry the onion in the heated margarine until golden brown.
2 Lightly beat the eggs.
3 Put all the ingredients into a greased casserole dish and bake at 190°C for 20 minutes or until set.

Serves 2–3.

Creamy Ribbons

Ingredients

150 g ribbon pasta (tagliatelle)
50 g diced bacon
1 tsp oil
2 eggs
1 tbsp cream or low-fat natural yoghurt
50 g grated cheese
½ tsp freshly ground black pepper

Method

1 Boil pasta in a large saucepan of salted water for 15-20 minutes.
2 Gently fry the bacon in oil until fat is transparent. Drain off excess fat.
3 Beat eggs and add cream or yoghurt, cheese and pepper.
4 Drain the pasta and immediately toss it in the egg mixture allowing the heat of the pasta to cook the egg. Fold in bacon.

Serves 2–3.

Fish

Did you know?

In Britain we eat on average 150 g of fish per person per week compared to 1 kg of meat eaten per person per week. This means we eat six times as much meat as fish. As with other 'Eat Moderately' foods, fish is an important source of proteins and vitamins and minerals.

It is lower in fat and is more easily digested than meat, so for a healthy diet we would benefit from eating more fish, especially white fish, which is very low in fat.

Fish can be cooked in many ways:

Baked in the oven

Cooked on the barbecue

Steamed

Fried

Variety is available in fish. The different kinds of fish can be purchased in a variety of ways:

Fresh Fish

* Whole

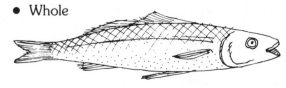

* Fillets

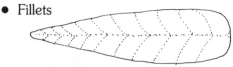

* Steaks

Frozen Fish

* Fillets
* Fishcakes
* Fish fingers
* Fish and chips
* Fish in breadcrumbs
* Fish in batter

Smoked Fish
Canned Fish

Dried Fish
Salted Fish
Pickled Fish

Because fish have quite a bland (mild) flavour they are often served with accompaniments (Check the meaning of **accompaniment** in the glossary.) Some of these are:

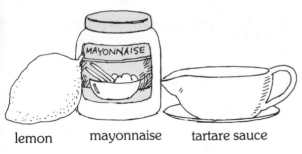

lemon mayonnaise tartare sauce

Buying Fish

When buying me make sure I am fresh. That's when I have a pleasant smell, my eyes are bright and my gills are red. I am not flabby when you touch me either.

Storing Fish

When you get me home, store me properly. Wrap me loosely in fresh paper or plastic wrap and put me in the refrigerator.

Recipes to Try

Fish in Cream Sauce

Any type of fresh fish can be used in this dish. Cook the fish first, by lightly poaching in water that has a little salt and pepper added to it. Canned fish can also be used.
You can serve this dish on toast, with rice, or in a pancake.

Cod

Plaice

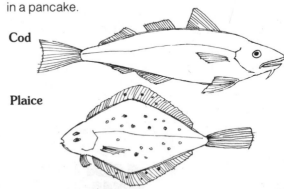

These are two types of fish that can be used.

Ingredients

50 g margarine
50 g flour
500 ml skimmed milk
1 tbsp lemon juice
500 g cooked or canned fish in large flakes
salt
freshly ground pepper
1 tbsp finely chopped parsley

Method

1 Heat the margarine in a heavy-based saucepan.
2 Stir in the flour and cook until smooth, about 2 minutes.
3 Slowly add the milk, continuing to stir.
4 Simmer for 2 minutes.
5 Mix the lemon juice into the fish and add to the cream sauce.
6 Add salt and pepper to taste, if desired.
7 Heat thoroughly, remove from the heat, and sprinkle with parsley.

Serves 4.

Variations of this recipe

Creamed Fish with Mushrooms

Add 100 g button mushrooms, sautéed in 1 tbsp margarine, to the sauce.

Creamed Fish with Tarragon

Add ¼ tsp dried tarragon, crumbled, with the milk.

Creamed Fish Florentine

Cook 1 large bunch spinach for about 5 minutes in the water left clinging to the leaves after washing. Drain well and put in a serving dish; spoon the creamed fish over the spinach.

Fish Cakes

Ingredients

250 g cod fillet
250 g potatoes
15 g sunflower margarine
salt and pepper
2 eggs
golden breadcrumbs
parsley
25 g wholemeal flour

Method

1 Cook fish and potatoes together by cooking potatoes in saucepan of boiling water, with the fish between two plates resting on top of saucepan.

2 Cook for 20 minutes.

3 Remove any bones from fish, mash with a fork.

4 Mash potatoes with margarine.

5 In a mixing bowl, mix fish, potatoes, chopped parsley and half a beaten egg.

6 Turn mixture out onto a floured table top, form into a roll.

7 Cut into six pieces. Shape into a round.

8 Coat each piece with egg and breadcrumbs.

9 Bake for 15 minutes in a hot oven 200°C mark 6.

Serves 3.

Questions about the recipe

a Suggest another method of cooking for fish cakes.

b Make a list of types of fish which are commonly eaten in Britain.

Braised Whiting or Plaice

Ingredients

2 whiting or plaice fillets
15 g margarine
25 g fresh wholemeal breadcrumbs
1 spring onion
1 tsp finely chopped parsley
2 tbsp chicken stock
2 tsp lemon juice

Method

1 Melt the margarine and brush it all over the fish. Dip the fish in the breadcrumbs.

2 Finely chop the spring onions and mix with the parsley. Sprinkle onions and parsley into the base of a shallow baking dish.

3 Place fish on top of onions.

4 Spoon the juice and stock around the fish — **not** over it. Bake in a moderately hot (220°C) oven for 15 minutes.

5 Carefully lift fish on to serving dishes and keep hot.

6 Pour liquid into a small pan and simmer until it has half evaporated. Pour the liquid over the fish.

Serves 2.

Crispy Baked Fish

Ingredients

250 g cod fillet or plaice
1 onion
1 tomato
2 slices wholemeal bread
50 g low fat Cheddar cheese
salt and pepper
pinch herbs

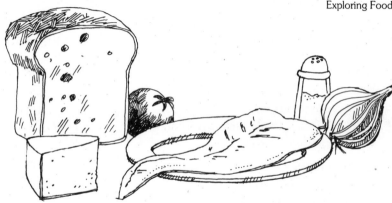

Method

1 Skin fish. Place in ovenproof dish.

2 Cover with thinly sliced tomato and onion.

3 Sprinkle with a pinch of salt, pepper and herbs.

4 To make topping, put bread and grated cheese in blender.

5 Sprinkle breadcrumb mixture over fish.

6 Bake in oven 190°C mark 5 for 30 minutes until crisp and browned on top.

Serves 2.

Pulses or Legumes

Legume is the scientific name for **pod**. Plants of the pea, bean and lentil families have pods containing seeds that we can eat. When they are young and green they are called vegetables. Vegetables belong in the 'Eat Most' group of foods.

When legumes become very ripe the pods dry up and split open, throwing the seeds or pulses (peas, beans and lentils) out. These mature seeds contain more of the nutrient protein than the green seeds and therefore belong in the 'Eat Moderately' group. These seeds can be dried and will keep for very long periods of time (years). In fact, in Egypt, the pyramids were found to contain little mounds of beans — food for the Pharaohs on their journey to the next world.

These dried seeds are a very good food. They are used by vegetarians and others, as a substitute for meat because they are some of the few 'Eat Moderately' foods that come from plants. The only other group of 'Eat Moderately' foods from plants is **nuts**, which we will look at later in this book.

- What is a vegetarian? From a class discussion write a definition of a vegetarian.

Types of Beans   **Types of Peas**

Uses in our diet:
- Soups
- Stews
- Spreads
- Salads
- Pastas
- Biscuits
- Pies

HARICOT BUTTER LIMA BLACK RED MUNG SOYA KIDNEY

CHICK SPLIT

— Soya beans can also be purchased as:
Soya flour
Soya milk
T.V.P. (imitation meat)

By mixing pulses with cereals, for example, baked beans on toast, vegetarians obtain what they need for growth and repair of body cells. Pulses also provide the body with fibre (meat does not contain fibre).

- Discuss other cereal/pulse combinations that a vegetarian might use.

What are Lentils?

Lentils were probably the first food ever cultivated by man. History tells us that they were enjoyed in the days of ancient Egypt, and that they spread to Europe and Asia.

Lentils are like peas and beans. They are now native to parts of India. Their seeds are red, brown or green. They taste the same as split peas and can be used in recipes instead of split peas — they do not need soaking before cooking whereas split peas do.

- Discuss how you use dried peas, beans and lentils in your home.

Workshop

1 Collect samples of as many dried peas, beans and lentils as you can. Examine them for differences in colour and shape.

2 Why do most recipes using pulses tell you to soak them before cooking?
Soak two or three samples of pulses overnight. Record any changes you observe.

3 Collect three recipes that contain dried peas, beans or lentils; copy or paste them into your book.

4 Prepare a buffet meal for your class using recipes your class collected, as well as those at the end of this workshop. Taste as many of the dishes as possible. Record your findings about the flavours and rate each recipe on a scale of 'poor' to 'very good'. Give reasons for your rating of each recipe.

5 Research the meaning of the word **pulses**.

6 Grow your own Bean Sprouts:
  a Soak 2 tbsp of seed (such as mung beans, alfalfa seeds or lentils) in water overnight.
  b Rinse well.
  c Place in a clean jar.
  d Cover the top with a piece of clean nylon stocking and hold in place with a rubber band.
  e Rinse the seeds well in water each morning and night for 2-5 days.
  f They are ready to eat when each sprout has grown to 2 cm or more in length.
  g The sprouts will keep in the refrigerator for several days.
  h Serve in a salad. Add chopped chicken and chives and French dressing to make an interesting sandwich filling or salad; add them to fried rice or other Chinese dishes.

- List any other uses for bean sprouts that you can think of.

Recipes to Try

Beans and Ham

Ingredients

400 g tin cannellini beans or borlotti beans
1 onion, chopped
2 celery sticks, chopped
400 g tin tomatoes
2 tbsp tomato purée
100 g chopped cooked ham – leave out for vegetarians
1 teasp basil or mixed herbs
2 teasp vegetable oil

Method

1 Put oil in saucepan; fry chopped onion for 5 minutes.
2 Add tomatoes and juice from tin.
3 Add chopped celery, tomato purée and herbs.
4 Add chopped ham (if used) and beans.
5 Simmer gently for 25 minutes with lid on saucepan.

Serves 2–3.

Chilli Con Carne

Ingredients

125 g lean minced beef
1 onion, chopped
400 g tin red kidney beans (drained)
1 tin tomato purée
½ tsp chilli powder

Method

1 Dry fry meat and onions in saucepan. Drain off any excess fat.
2 Add tomato purée, chilli powder and 125 ml water; simmer gently for 20 minutes.
3 Add beans to the meat mixture and simmer for a further 20 minutes.
4 Serve with rice and a green salad.

Note: chilli powder is HOT — add carefully.

Serves 2.

Nuts

Nuts have been used since the earliest of times in a large variety of dishes. They are rich in protein and oils and contain vitamins and fibre. Nuts have many uses in cookery all over the world:

- Egyptians and Iranians use ground almonds and pine nuts to thicken sauces, as well as using them whole in stuffings for lamb, mutton, chicken and vegetables.

- Greeks put lots of walnuts between syrupy pastry to make Baklava.

- Indian dishes are decorated with almonds or cashew nuts, and coconut is an important part of curries.

- In Africa, peanuts are used in all sorts of stews.

- In Europe, chestnuts are used for savoury and sweet dishes, and you can buy hot roasted chestnuts from take-away food carts in the streets of Greece and other parts of Europe.

- Pecan nut pie is a famous American pie.

- Peanuts are the most commonly used nut in Britain. You can buy them in the shell, raw, roasted, salted, as peanut butter or peanut oil.

Workshop

1 Discuss how you use nuts in your family meals.
2 Find out which country grows the most nuts. What type of nuts are grown there?
3 Look in the library and make a sketch of a peanut plant in your book.
4 If you can organise a fire in an open fireplace or barbecue pit, roast some chestnuts and eat them when they pop open.
5 **Nutty Puzzle**
   Solve this crossword puzzle:

Clues

Across

2 Pale green nuts from the Middle East.

5 Used as decoration in some Indian dishes.

8 Sugar coated, chocolate coated, or used as a garnish.

10 Pecan nuts are used in America to make a ....

11 This puzzle is about ....

13 Nuts must be cracked .... before we can eat them.

16 Chopped nuts can be used for ....

18 Nuts can be served with foods like beans, broccoli, corn, lettuce, etc. These plant foods are called ....

Down

1 A nut from a tree we decorate at Christmas.

3 In Africa peanuts are used in all sorts of ....

4 Used to describe eye colour.

6 Type of nut which can be pickled.

7 Grows on a palm tree.

9 The most common nut in Britain.

12 The outer covering of a nut.

14 Nuts used in an American dessert.

15 Nuts are often used to give this food flavour and texture, or to decorate it.

17 Made from nuts and used for frying food.

6 Organise a nut tasting session. This can be done in two ways: your teacher can arrange to get a variety of nuts or, each class member can bring a different kind of nut. Design a record sheet similar to your cheese testing chart on p. 74 to record your results.

Recipes to Try

Banana Nut Salad

Ingredients

1 large red apple
50 g diced celery
60 ml mayonnaise (low fat)
2 medium sized bananas
4 lettuce leaves
50 g peanuts

Method

1 Dice apple into 1 cm pieces and toss with celery and mayonnaise.

2 Peel bananas and cut into slices.

3 Add to apple mixture and toss lightly.

4 Arrange lettuce on serving plates and fill leaves with apple mixture.

5 Sprinkle with nuts.

Serves 4.

Stuffed Tomatoes

Ingredients

1 large tomato
1 tbsp cashew nuts (Other nuts could be used)
1 piece celery, 10-15 cms long
salt and pepper to taste
(Note: salt is not necessary if nuts are already salted.)

Method

1   Carefully slice a piece from top of tomato.
2   Scoop out the pulp of the tomato and chop finely.
3   Slice the celery finely.
4   Mix the nuts, tomato and celery together and add seasoning.
5   Spoon mixture back into the tomato and replace the caps.
6   Bake in a moderate oven for 10-15 minutes or serve cold without baking as a salad.

Serves 1.

Lemon Crunchies

Ingredients

50 g margarine
75 g castor sugar
1 tsp grated lemon rind
½ egg
150 g S.R. flour
25 g walnuts, crushed
25 g sultanas

Method

1   Cream margarine and sugar and lemon rind.
2   Beat egg and mix in well.
3   Add flour and mix thoroughly.
4   Add nuts and sultanas and mix through evenly.
5   Form into balls the size of a walnut.
6   Place on a tray leaving space for spreading. Press to about 1 cm thick with a fork. Bake in moderate oven (190°C, mark 5) for 20–25 minutes until golden.

Peanut Cookies

Ingredients

50 g S.R. flour
50 g S.R. wholemeal flour
50 g sunflower margarine
25 g sugar
50 g unsalted peanuts (skins removed)
4–6 tsps skimmed milk

Method

1   Put flour, margarine and sugar into a mixing bowl and rub together until the mixture looks like breadcrumbs.
2   Add approximately 4–6 teaspoons milk to make a stiff dough.
3   Roll out dough on a floured surface to about ½ cm thick, cut into rounds with a biscuit cutter.
4   Place on a greased baking tray, brush with milk and press a few roughly chopped peanuts onto the top of each biscuit.
5   Bake in oven 180°C mark 4 for 10–15 minutes until crisp and golden brown.

Makes 12.

'Eat Least' Foods

Fats, oils and sugar can be considered as 'extras' in your diet.

The body needs fats, but we get enough from the 'Eat Moderately' and 'Eat Most' groups of food. If you want butter, margarine or oil, you should only have ½-1 tablespoon daily.

Sugar such as refined, brown or raw cane sugar, syrups and honey are used by the body for energy. The **best** energy sources are the 'Eat Most' foods.

If you decide to add sugar to your diet, do so in small amounts. Remember how it appears on the Healthy Diet Pyramid before you eat.

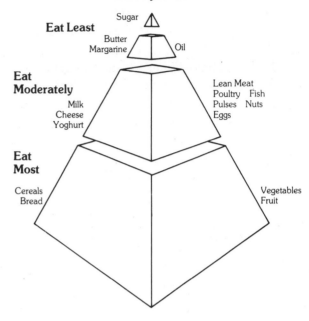

The Healthy Diet Pyramid

Butter, Margarine, Fats, Oils

Vitamins A, D, E and K are supplied by these foods. They are also a source of energy.
Fats in our diet come from:

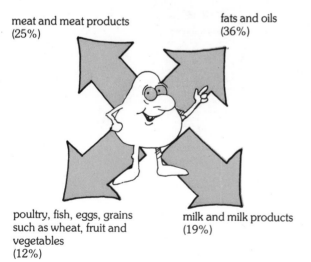

meat and meat products (25%)

fats and oils (36%)

poultry, fish, eggs, grains such as wheat, fruit and vegetables (12%)

milk and milk products (19%)

There are two main sources of fats and oils:
Animal

Pigs
Cows
Sheep
Beef
} Lard
Milk Products
Dripping from Cooked Meats
Suet — white fat from
around the organs
of the animals

Vegetable

Soya Beans
Oil Palm
Coconuts
Peanuts
Safflower
Olives
Sunflowers
Sesame Seeds
Maize

97

Did you know?

- Margarine is an oil-based spread that was originally made to be used instead of butter. It is made mainly from vegetable oils and skimmed milk.

- 1 tablespoon of butter, oil, or margarine daily is enough to meet your body's needs.

- As large amounts of fat in your diet can cause heart diseases, it is *important* to limit the amount of fat in your daily diet. Many snack foods have fat in them.

What type of snacks can you eat that do not contain a lot of fat or oil?

Workshop

1   Make your own Butter.

Ingredients

300 ml of double cream
a very clean 500 ml jar with a screw-top lid.

Method

1   Stir the cream gently and then pour it into the jar.

2   Screw on the lid.

3   Shake the jar constantly for 12 minutes. (What else could you use instead of this method?) You should end up with butter and a liquid which is called *buttermilk*.

4   Pour off the buttermilk. Place some in a glass and try it.

5   Try your butter in the **Savoury Bread** recipe at the end of this workshop.

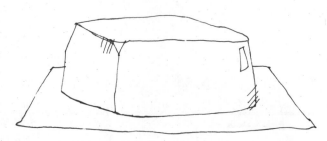

2   Unjumble the words below to reveal some sources of vegetable oils. Write them in your book.

a	APNTEU	d	FSNULWEOR
b	AZIME	e	SAMEES
c	RWFASFLOE	f	ABYSOAEN

3   Research what the term **shortening** means.

4 Complete this sentence in your book.
Butter, fats and oils supply the body with ....

5 ● Discuss: How can you be sure your diet has a suitable supply of fat?

6 Complete this crossword puzzle.

Clues

Across

3 A vegetable source of oils.
5 Liquid fat.
7 Fats and sugars belong to the — least part of the Healthy Diet Pyramid.
8 A spread made mainly from vegetable oils and skimmed milk.
9 A part of the body that could become diseased if the diet is high in fat.

Down

1 It can be spread on bread.
2 Oily seeds.
4 At the top of the pyramid.
6 White cooking fat.
8 A cereal source of oil.

7 Fats Search. Find the Hidden Fats.

Fats can be visible or invisible. *Invisible* fats are those which we can see like butter, margarine and cooking oil. *Invisible* or *hidden* fats are those which are contained in these foods: egg yolk, fish, seeds and nuts, the fat which may be left in meat once the visible fat is trimmed away, and fat in commercial products. Therefore we may eat a lot of invisible fats without realising it. Look at the ingredients labels on foods and see if you can find the hidden fats. Food labels list the ingredients in order of quantity, so the ingredient present in the largest quantity is first on the list. This gives you some idea of how much fat is in the food.

Make a list of foods which contain invisible fats. Discuss your findings with the rest of the class. Make a classroom display of your results.

Recipe to Try

Savoury Bread

Be creative — make your own tasty butter. You can
add ground black pepper, garlic, fresh herbs,
anchovies, parsley, shrimp, or anything else you
can think of, to your freshly made butter.

1   Take an oblong roll.
2   Cut it into slices almost all the way through.
3   Spread both sides of each slice with your butter.
4   Wrap in tin foil.
5   Cook in a moderate oven for 10-15 minutes.

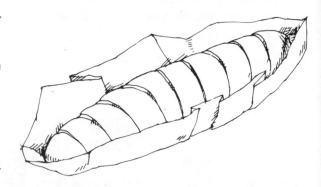

Sugar

Did you know ?

- Sugar is:
  sucrose from sugar cane and sugar beet
  fructose from fruit
  lactose from milk
  honey from bees.

- Too much sugar **added** to food may cause
  tooth decay or heart disease.

- **Added** sugar is:
  Extra sucrose (white sugar, brown
        sugar, raw sugar, syrup and
        treacle)
  Extra honey
  Extra fructose
  Extra lactose mixed into food for flavour
            or to preserve food.
  Extra dextrose or glucose syrup in
        manufactured foods.

- We eat an average of 44 kg of sugar a year.

- 70% of the sugar we eat is hidden in
  manufactured foods, such as soft drinks,
  cordial, biscuits, tinned fruit, breakfast
  cereals, sauces and prepared fruit juices.

- The most common form of sugar is sucrose
  (white sugar) which comes from sugar cane
  and sugar beet.

Workshop

1   **Sugar Search:** Sugar is added to the foods that we eat every day.
Check your shelves at home and make a list of all the foods that contain
sugar. How many foods did you find? Discuss this with your class.
Compare your results. (You may have done a similar exercise in the lesson
on snacks. If so, look back at your findings.)

2   Practical Exercise No. 15.

YOU DECIDE!

Practical Exercise No. 15
Food as a Treat

Aim
- To understand that sweet foods are an 'extra' in our daily diet. They should be regarded as a treat, not as a regular part of the diet.

Equipment
Top of an egg carton, or a 2 litre ice-cream container, or a large jar with a lid, coloured paper or foil; plastic wrap; ribbon or flowers or gift tie.

Procedure
a Cover the container with coloured paper. If using a jar, cover the lid and decorate the glass with cut-out shapes. Keep plastic wrap, ribbon etc. for later.

b Make a batch of biscuits using the **Quick Biscuits** recipe at the end of the workshop or one that your teacher gives you.

c When the biscuits are cool, pack them neatly and attractively into your container and cover or wrap in cling film.

d Decorate with a bow or flowers or cut-out shapes.

e Present your biscuits as a treat to your family or a friend.
If your class visits an elderly folks home in your district, take the biscuits as a treat.

Recipes to Try

Quick Biscuits

Ingredients

50 g coconut
100 g S.R. flour (white or wholemeal)
70 g melted margarine
100 g sugar
½ egg

- What is the best way to halve a raw egg?

Method

1 Collect ingredients.
2 Melt margarine in a saucepan over a low heat. Be careful not to burn the margarine.
3 Place all the ingredients except the margarine in a bowl.
4 Add the margarine and mix till you have a smooth dough
5 Grease a tray.
6 Carefully roll the dough into small balls about the size of a 50p coin. Place on tray, spacing them out to allow for spreading. To make them fancy you can put a piece of cherry or nut on the centre of each biscuit.
7 Bake in the oven at 180°C mark 4 for 15 minutes or until golden brown.
8 Allow to cool.

Feather Sponge

Ingredients

3 eggs
75 g wholemeal flour
75 g raw cane sugar

Method

1. Break eggs into mixing bowl; add sugar.
2. Whisk eggs and sugar until mixture is very thick.
3. Fold in flour carefully – do not over stir.
4. Pour mixture into two greased and lined 18cm sandwich tins.
5. Bake at 180°C mark 4 for 20 minutes until risen and spongy. Allow to cool. Fill with a little jam or fruit purée.

Feather Topping

Prepare the following glacé icing:
100 g icing sugar (sifted)
3 tsp water   } Mix together

1. Put 1 tbsp of the icing into a piping bag with a small plain (No. 2) pipe.
2. Sift 2 tsp cocoa into the remaining icing and mix well. You may need to add a few more drops of water — check with your teacher.
3. Spread the chocolate icing onto your cold sponge cake, taking care not to let it dribble over the sides.
4. Work very quickly as both lots of icing must be wet for this to work.

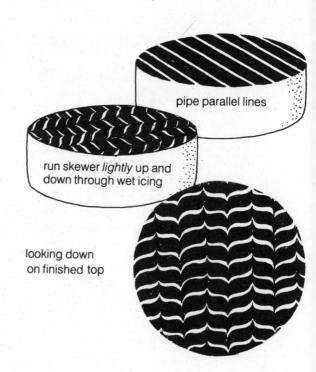

pipe parallel lines

run skewer *lightly* up and down through wet icing

looking down on finished top

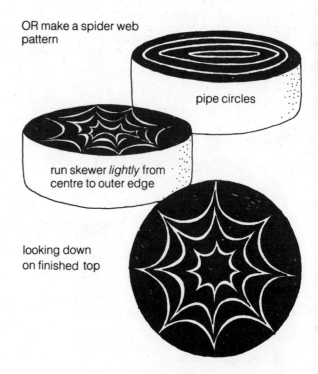

OR make a spider web pattern

pipe circles

run skewer *lightly* from centre to outer edge

looking down on finished top

Note: Other colours could be used for icing.

102

Part 2 Evaluation Test

1 Copy this table into your book.

'Eat Most' group	'Eat Moderately' group	'Eat Least' group

Place the following foods under the headings that they belong to on the Healthy Diet Pyramid.

eggs   fish   butter   apples   tomatoes
bread   spaghetti   nuts   sugar   chicken

Choose the correct answers for questions 2 to 11. Write them in your book.

2 Wheat and other cereal grains are the .... of grass plants.
   a   leaves
   b   seeds
   c   stems
   d   roots

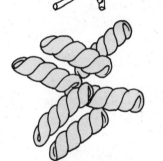

3 The cereal grown in the greatest amount in Britain is ....
   a   wheat
   b   barley
   c   oats
   d   rye

4 Spaghetti, macaroni, cannelloni are all forms of ....
   a   pulses
   b   rice
   c   pasta
   d   soup

5 'Long grain', 'short grain' and 'brown' are all types of ....
   a   rice
   b   wheat
   c   oats
   d   barley

6 Bread rises because of the ....
   a   yeast
   b   flour
   c   salt
   d   sugar

7 One type of milk which is unsuitable for lengthy storage is .... milk.
   a   powdered
   b   tinned
   c   pasteurised
   d   condensed

8 Which of the following is not a dairy product?
   a yoghurt
   b flour
   c cream
   d cheese

9 Meat is a major source of .... in our diets.
   a protein
   b minerals
   c carbohydrates
   d fats

10 Which animal does pork come from?
   a pig
   b turkey
   c cow
   d sheep

11 Which of the following is often served with fish?
   a lemon
   b orange
   c grapefruit
   d lime

12 What is the difference between butter and margarine?

13 a Why is protein important in the body?
    b List five food sources of protein.

14 Match the sugar to its source:
    sucrose   milk
    fructose   fruit
    lactose   cane sugar

15 List five ways you can cook potatoes.

In your book, write **true** or **false** for questions 16 to 20.

16 Fruits contain a natural sugar called fructose.

17 Fruits supply the body with vitamins and minerals.

18 Meat from the legs of an animal is more likely to be tough than meat from the rump.

19 Britons eat 140 g of meat a day.

20 Meat belongs to the 'Eat Most' group on the Healthy Diet Pyramid.

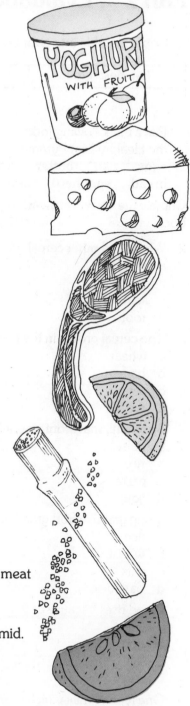

Part 3 Food and Me

8 My Body and Food

Why Do I Need Food?

In a motor car the fuel gauge shows you when the car needs petrol.

When you feel hungry, your body is telling you that it needs fuel. Food is fuel for the body. Food is needed to keep the body working and growing.

Food

— keeps bones and teeth strong

— keeps eyes healthy

— helps protect against illness

— keeps the skin healthy

— keeps the body growing

— helps the body repair cuts and wounds

— keeps the body supplied with energy

- Can you name some other ways in which the body uses food?

- How does your body stay healthy?
  Not only does your body need lots of different foods, it needs more of some foods than of others to maintain a healthy you.

- Can you remember from the last chapter which foods your body needs the most, which foods it needs in moderation and which foods it needs the least?

Workshop

Practical Exercise No. 16
Meal Planning

Aim
- To plan and prepare a healthy meal
- To learn how to manage food ordering

Procedure

a With a partner or in a group of four, plan a meal that will help to keep you healthy. Some recipes below or elsewhere in this book might help you to plan your meal.

b When you have planned your meal, make a list of the amounts of *all* ingredients you will need. Write them down in columns under these headings:

Supermarket	Butcher	Greengrocer	Dairy

c Hand in your completed list to your teacher. This list is called a **food order.**

d Prepare the planned meal in your next lesson.

Evaluation

Copy this diagram into your book.
Write next to 'a', 'b' and 'c' the ingredients you used in your meal.

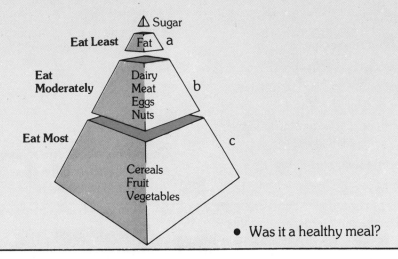

⚠ Sugar

Eat Least — Fat — a

Eat Moderately — Dairy Meat Eggs Nuts — b

Eat Most — Cereals Fruit Vegetables — c

- Was it a healthy meal?

Recipes to Try

Wholemeal Pancakes

Ingredients

100 g wholemeal flour
250 ml skimmed milk
1 egg
1 tbsp sunflower oil

Method

1 Put flour into a mixing bowl, make a well in the centre.

2 Put the egg into the well in the flour, beat the egg mixing in the flour gradually.

3 Add milk, slowly beating well to make a smooth batter.

4 To cook pancakes: heat a small quantity of sunflower oil in a frying pan. Pour in a little of the batter, tip the pan to spread the batter evenly. Turn the pancake over when it has set on the surface and cook until brown on the other side.

5 Serve with fruit purée and a scoop of ice-cream.

To make fruit purée

Cook fruit very gently in a little water, ripe fruit needs no sugar, firm fruit might need 1 tsp sugar per piece of fruit. When cooked place in blender or rub through a sieve. Serve hot or cold.

Makes 8–10 pancakes

Questions about the recipe

a Which piece of small electrical equipment could be used to make the batter?

b Which is the best type of frying pan to use for cooking pancakes?

c Suggest some savoury fillings for pancakes.

d What does **purée** mean? If you are unsure look up the glossary at the back of this book.

Kebabs and Beefy Rice

Ingredients

2 frankfurters or low fat sausages
2 bacon rashers
10 pineapple pieces
2 tsp tomato sauce
1 tsp pineapple juice
2–4 skewers
1 beef stock cube
150 g brown rice
500 ml hot water

Method

1 Crumble beef cube into water in a saucepan. Bring to the boil and add rice.

2 Simmer for 25 minutes until rice is tender.

3 Cut frankfurters into 2–2½ cm lengths. Remove rind from bacon.

4 Thread frankfurter, bacon and pineapple onto skewers.

5 Place under a hot grill, turn frequently until cooked (about 12 minutes).

6 Mix sauce and juice together, brush over food on skewer; return to grill for a few minutes

7 Serve beefy rice on a warm plate; slide food from skewer onto rice.

Serves 2.

Questions about the recipe

a What are the differences between brown rice and polished rice?

b From which animal do we get bacon?

c What are the safety rules to remember when using a grill?

Chow Mein

Ingredients

180 g minced steak
1 tbsp vermicelli
1 chicken stock cube
200 ml hot water
1½ tbsp rice
1 stalk celery
½ sliced onion
75 g shredded cabbage
50 g sliced green beans
1 tbsp tomato sauce
¼ tsp curry powder

Method

1 Place meat, water, vermicelli, rice and stock cube (crumbled) in saucepan. Mix well and simmer for 20 minutes.
2 Add all other ingredients and simmer 10 minutes longer.

Serves 2.

Peach and Orange Salad

Ingredients

4 lettuce leaves
4 orange slices
4 slices canned peaches
1 stick celery
4 cucumber slices
1 spring onion

Salad dressing
1 tbsp mayonnaise
1 tbsp low-fat yoghurt
2 tsp chopped parsley
¼ tsp grated orange rind

Method

1 Wash celery and cut into 8 cm lengths. Slice into very thin strips leaving one end intact. Put into iced water until celery curls.
2 Wash lettuce and shake dry.
3 Wash spring onion, remove roots and slice finely.
4 Arrange all fruit and vegetables neatly in a lettuce leaf on serving plate.
5 Combine all salad dressing ingredients, serve in a separate little glass dish with a spoon for all to share.

Serves 4.

Other recipes you might like to try for Practical Exercise No. 16:
Spaghetti Bolognaise, page 81.
Chicken Tacos, page 80.
Coleslaw, page 19.
Apple Edam Open Sandwich, page 124.
Fruit Salad, page 63.
Melon Dessert, page 121.
Instant Breakfast Drink, page 115.

How Does My Body Use Food?

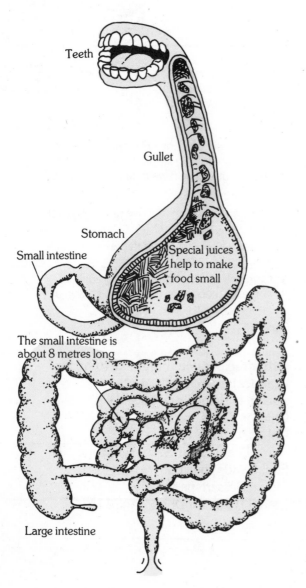

Teeth

Gullet

Stomach

Small intestine

Special juices help to make food small

The small intestine is about 8 metres long

Large intestine

Teeth   They bite, cut, tear and grind food.

Mouth   Food is mixed with saliva and swallowed.

Gullet   Chewed food is lowered into the stomach.

Stomach   Food is made 'soupy'. The inside walls of the stomach and intestines are a bit like carpet which is thickest in the small intestine.

More special juices are added in the **Small Intestine** and food is made into really tiny bits that the body can use. These tiny bits of food are so small that they can go right through the walls of the small intestine into the blood so that the body can use food for all the 'workings' and growing we talked about in the last lesson.

The bits of food which your body cannot use move into the **Large Intestine**. Any water left in the food that your body wants to keep goes through the walls of the large intestine and becomes part of the blood.

- All this activity is called **Digestion**.
- The mouth, the gullet, the stomach, the small intestine and the large intestine all together are called the **Digestive System**.

One important part of food that doesn't go through intestine walls into the blood is **fibre**. Fibre is important because it helps the food you eat move smoothly and easily through the digestive system. It does this by acting like a sponge which soaks up water, making a soft mass of food for the muscles in the intestine walls to push along. A food mass that is too solid might cause damage to the walls of the large intestine.

The best source of dietary fibre is wheat.
- Which other foods give us fibre?
- Make a list of these foods.
- On which part of the Healthy Diet Pyramid do these foods belong?

Workshop

1   This is about where your digestive system is placed in your body. Copy this drawing into your book. Colour in the digestive system showing a *yellow* gullet, a *green* stomach, a *red* small intestine and a *blue* large intestine.

2   Below are some recipes which contain lots of fibre. You might like to use one of these recipes in class. Write your chosen recipe into your book and underline all the ingredients containing fibre.

Recipes to Try

Oatmeal Pancakes

Ingredients

75 g wholemeal flour
75 g rolled oats
1½ tps baking powder
¼ tsp salt (optional)
1 beaten egg
1½ tsp oil
1½ tsp honey
200 ml milk

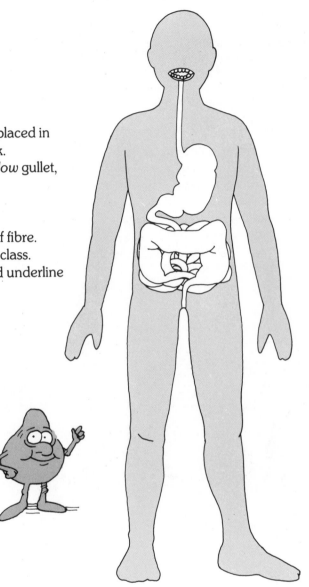

Method

1   Mix dry ingredients.
2   Add all other ingredients and blend well.
3   Heat a little oil in a frying pan. Add 1 tbsp of the mixture to pan. Turn when edges begin to dry.
4   Serve with stewed fruit or yoghurt

Makes 8 pancakes.

Banana Bran Cakes

Ingredients

100 g S.R. wholemeal flour
1 tbsp bran
50 g brown sugar
1 egg (beaten lightly)
1 mashed ripe banana
75 g natural yoghurt (½ carton)
1 tbsp vegetable oil

Method

1 Stir dry ingredients together.

2 Make a well in the centre of flour. Pour in banana and all other ingredients and stir until just moistened.

3 Half fill 8 paper cake cases with the mixture.

4 Quickly put into oven and bake at 200°C mark 6 for 15 minutes.

Soda Bread

Ingredients

100 g S.R. wholemeal flour
100 g S.R. white flour
20 g bran
½ tsp bicarbonate of soda
1 tsp cream of tartar
125 ml milk and water (½ and ½)
15 g margarine

Method

1 Mix the flours in a bowl.

2 Rub in the margarine.

3 Stir in thoroughly the bicarbonate of soda and cream of tartar.

4 Mix in the milk and water to make a soft dough.

5 Turn onto a floured worksurface and knead gently for 30 seconds until smooth.

6 Shape into a round 5 cm deep, mark into quarters.

7 Place on a greased baking tray and bake for 30 minutes at 200°C mark 6, until a deep golden colour.

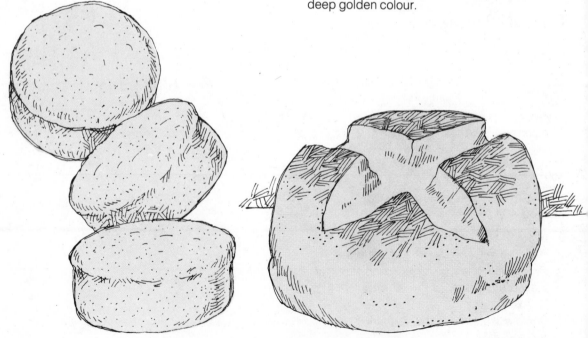

9   A Day with Food

Breakfast

Do you start the day in a hurry,
Leaving home in a rush?
Does the morning go on forever
'Cause you've no food to last 'til lunch?

Do you fidget and wriggle and scratch
As you sit in your morning classes?
Is it hard to think about your work
So that all your marks are passes?

That brain computer needs breakfast foods
To help you to think and smile.
Start your day the healthy way,
And sit and eat a while.

Eating breakfast is the smart way to start the day. A morning meal gives your body the fuel it needs for a busy day.

Breakfast is especially important because usually many hours have passed since the last meal was eaten.

If you are short of time, or cannot face food first thing in the morning, pack a snack breakfast and eat it later — walking to school or on the bus. It is not really any trouble to prepare:

1   Collect a plastic bag or paper bag.

2   Go into the kitchen and look in places where food is kept.

3   Put something in the bag for later.

4   Some ideas:

Fruit   Nuts   Bread   Cheese   Hard-boiled Egg   Dry Biscuits   Dried Fruit   Salad

Not a perfect start to the day, but better than no breakfast at all!

Workshop

1 What kind of foods do you think are eaten at breakfast time by people who organise a sensible breakfast? Make a list of these foods on the board.

2 Work your way through the next practical exercise.

Practical Exercise No. 17
Breakfast Survey

a Conduct a survey of other classes at school and find out:
   — how many people eat breakfast,
   — what people eat for breakfast.
   (See page 20 for notes on surveys.)

b What percentage of the pupils you surveyed ate breakfast?

c What were the three most popular breakfast foods?
   Think back to your class discussion in Activity 1 of this workshop and the list of breakfast foods you made on the board. Were the three popular foods from your survey on that list?

d How do these three popular breakfast foods work for the body?

e In what ways has your survey been helpful in teaching you about breakfasts?

f What was the *aim* of this practical exercise?

3 Make yourself a healthy breakfast to try at school. There are some recipes at the end of this workshop that you might like to use.

4 How many cereals can you find? Use each letter once only.

Breakfast Recipes to Try

Fruit Smoothie

Ingredients

1 banana (or any other fruit you like)
375 ml unsweetened pineapple juice
(or any other juice you like)
125 ml natural yoghurt

Method

1 Mash banana well (some other fruits might need grating).
2 Add juice and yoghurt and mix in a food processor, blender or beat with an egg beater.
3 On a hot morning add some ice.

Serves 1.

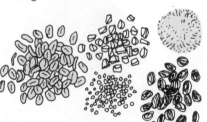

Muesli

Ingredients

400 g rolled oats
50 g unprocessed bran
200 g of a mixture of any of the following sunflower seeds, sesame seeds, chopped nuts, sultanas or other dried fruit, coconut

Method

1 Mix all ingredients together and take home for family breakfasts. Store in an airtight jar.
2 If you like your muesli **toasted**, spread the rolled oats on to a piece of foil under a medium heat grill. Toast the oats for one or two minutes, pull out grill, stir the oats so most turn over. Grill again until just golden brown.
   Watch the grill as the oats will burn if left too long.
3 If you like it **roasted**, spread it on a tray and bake in the oven at 160°C mark 3 for about 1 hour — stir up ingredients on tray every 15 minutes.

Instant Breakfast Drink

Ingredients

125 ml fruit juice, any flavour
1 egg
125 ml natural yoghurt

Method

Shake all together in a screw-top jar or mix in a blender.
Serves 1.

Scrambled Eggs with Cheese

Ingredients

3 eggs
25 g grated cheese
3 tbsp milk
a pinch pepper and salt
1 tsp margarine
2 slices toast

Method

1 Beat eggs, milk, pepper and salt together.
2 Melt margarine in saucepan or frying pan.
3 Pour in egg-milk mixture.
4 Stir until mixture thickens but is still moist.
5 Sprinkle grated cheese over hot mixture and allow it to melt.
6 Serve on toast.

Serves 2.

Questions about the recipe

a If you ate this for breakfast which part of the Healthy Diet Pyramid would you need very little of for the rest of the day?

b Describe how the mixture changed as you cooked it.

Rolled Oats with Nuts and Sultanas

Ingredients

50 g quick oats
125 ml milk
125 ml water
2 tbsp unprocessed bran (optional)
pinch of salt
50 g sultanas
50 g peanuts (or if you don't like 'crunchy' porridge, add ½ a finely sliced apple instead)

Method

1 Mix oats, bran, milk, water and salt in a saucepan.

2 Bring to the boil, stirring frequently.

3 Add sultanas and nuts.

4 Simmer, stirring constantly for 5-10 minutes.

5 Cover saucepan, remove from heat and let it stand for 3 minutes.

6 Serve hot with milk or yoghurt.

Serves 2.

Snacks

All foods eaten daily become part of you. Foods eaten as snacks or tasted while cooking are a part of your daily diet.

It is quite natural for teenagers to get hungry between meals because they are growing quickly. Teenagers who are active and who run about a lot need snacks.

When deciding what to eat for a snack you should still remember this:

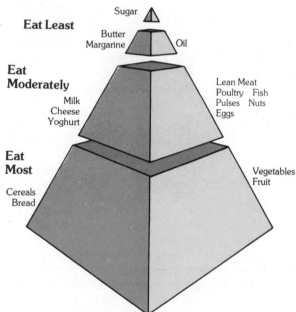

There are usually healthy snacks at home in the cupboard, for example, a handful of dried fruit, or in the refrigerator, for example, a glass of milk or a piece of fruit.

- Discuss with your class *when* people eat snacks.

- Discuss places *where* you might buy snacks. Where are they the most expensive? (for example, shows, theatres, parks)

- Discuss the types of foods eaten as snacks. Make a list of these.
  How many of the foods listed belong on the 'top' of the Healthy Diet Pyramid?

Workshop

1 Have a snack party and invite a class from a neighbouring school to join you.

2 Several snacks are sketched below. Copy the table below into your book. Select the most sensible and most economical snack for each of the occasions listed in the left hand column and give one reason for each choice.

Note: To do this exercise well you must research the cost of the snacks.

Occasion	Snack Choice	Reason
a A summer picnic		
b A bike ride		
c A snack after school		
d Cinema		
e A long bus trip		
f Mid-morning snack		
g Birthday party		

3 Practical Exercise No. 18.

YOU DECIDE!

Practical Exercise No. 18
The Snack Shop

Aim
- To help you to make decisions about snacks

Procedure
a Keep a record of how much money you spend on snacks during the next week. (Keep a pencil and paper in your pocket and jot down the cost each time you visit the 'snack shop'.)

b Total the amount spent for one week.

c In your book, work out the following sum:

Amount spent on
snacks for one week × **52** Weeks in a year = ...

d Think of all the things you want that you might be able to buy with that money, e.g. a bike, a cassette player.

4 What is your personal list of economical healthy snacks?

Snack Recipes to Try

Popcorn

Ingredients

1 tbsp oil
50 g popping corn

Method

1 Heat oil in a saucepan or frying pan with lid.
2 Add corn and shake pan gently over heat with the lid on.
3 Keep shaking the pan over the heat until you can no longer hear the corn popping.
4 Remove from heat; discard any unpopped pieces.
5 Eat it as it is, drizzle melted butter over or sprinkle with a little icing sugar.

Corn and Ham Scramble

Ingredients

1 egg
1 tbsp skimmed milk
15 g sunflower margarine
25 g cooked ham finely chopped
25 g sweetcorn
pepper
1 thick slice wholemeal bread

Method

1 Toast bread on both sides, spread with a little margarine, put on a plate and place in a low oven to keep hot.
2 Beat egg and milk together add a pinch of pepper.
3 Melt a knob of margarine in a small non-stick saucepan, turn heat down and pour eggs into the saucepan add ham and sweetcorn and scramble until just set.
4 Pile mixture onto hot toast.

Serves 1.

Cheese Biscuits

Ingredients

100 g S.R. wholemeal flour
25 g sunflower margarine
50 g low fat Cheddar cheese
3 tbsps skimmed milk

Method

1 Put flour and margarine in mixing bowl.
2 Rub together until mixture resembles breadcrumbs.
3 Add finely grated cheese.
4 Stir in enough milk to make a stiff dough.
5 Roll out on a floured surface.
6 Cut into biscuits or straws.
7 Place on a greased baking tray and bake in oven at 200°C mark 6 for 10–15 minutes.

Makes 15–20 biscuits.

Banana Cake

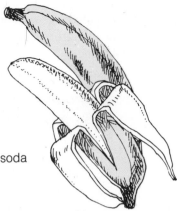

Ingredients

100 g sugar
40 g margarine
1 egg
2 large ripe bananas
225 g S.R. flour
3 tbsp milk
½ tsp bicarbonate of soda

Method

1 Soften margarine, add sugar and beat until creamy.
2 Add egg and beat until light in colour.
3 Mash banana and add to mixture.
4 Sift flour. Add bicarbonate of soda to milk and stir gently.
5 Add flour and milk alternately to the margarine and sugar, stirring gently.
6 Bake in a greased ring tin at 180°C mark 4 for about 30 minutes.

   Note Wholemeal S.R. flour could be used.

Dental Health

One reason why you should avoid sugary snacks is because they encourage your teeth to develop holes.

The sweet foods you might want to eat are better eaten at meal times with other foods, especially with dairy foods or with green leafy vegetables.

On *average,* we eat more than half a kilogram of sugar *each week* in all sorts of foods:

- Where does all this sugar come from?
- How do you think this figure of ½ kg per week was worked out?

Probably the most important feature of your face is your mouth and the smile it produces.

Unless this smile shows others a healthy, clean set of teeth, it might not be very helpful in making you look and feel good.

- Can you count how many teeth you have?
- How does this compare with the rest of the class?

A full set of teeth consists of 32 teeth.
Teeth have different shapes and sizes and do different work.

If you could cut a tooth in half it would look a bit like this:

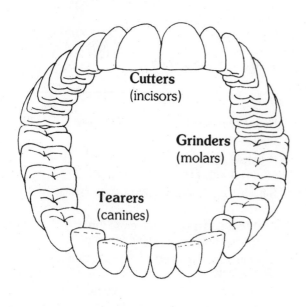

Cutters
(incisors)

Grinders
(molars)

Tearers
(canines)

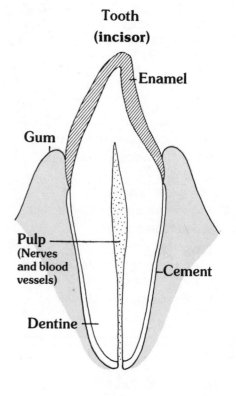

Tooth
(incisor)

Enamel

Gum

Pulp
(Nerves
and blood
vessels)

Cement

Dentine

Teeth need to be cleaned after you eat.

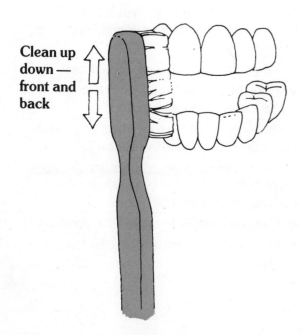

Clean up down — front and back

When sugary foods are eaten often and teeth are not cleaned, holes start to develop in the tooth **enamel**.

Tooth enamel is the hardest substance in your body but it can still be worn out.

● How do holes form in teeth?

A colourless film called **plaque** forms on teeth. **Bacteria** collect on the plaque. These bacteria need food. The food they use is the sugar that you leave on and in between your teeth. As they feed on this sugar, they give off an acid which causes holes to form in tooth enamel. This happens in much the same sort of way as rust holes form in metal.

● Are your teeth healthy?

Workshop

1 Look at all the food labels in the Home Economics Room, or in your kitchen at home. List all the foods which contain sugar. Do they all taste sweet?

How might this information influence you in the foods you choose to eat? (You may have done this exercise in Chapter 7 on Sugar. If so, look back at your notes.)

2 Try making a 'no added sugar' dessert. Some recipes are suggested below.

Recipes to Try

Fruit Sticks

You will need some wooden skewers. Thread pieces of fruit, e.g. watermelon, strawberries, cherries, bananas, oranges, etc. on to skewers and enjoy munching them.

Apple Dessert

Ingredients

2 tbsp semolina
375 ml milk
2 tbsp sultanas
1 grated apple (eating apple)
a few drops of lemon essence

Melon Dessert

Spoon cottage cheese or low fat cream cheese into wedges of honey-dew melon or cantaloupe. Decorate with a fresh strawberry, a cherry or a slice of kiwi fruit.

Method

1 Peel and core the apple. Grate it into a saucepan.

2 Add all other ingredients to apple and stir over a medium heat until mixture boils and thickens.

3 Pour into 4 wetted moulds and allow to set.

4 When set turn out into dessert bowls. Garnish with a piece of fresh fruit if desired.

Serves 4.

Questions about the recipe

a Why did the mixture thicken when it boiled?

b This dessert tastes slightly sweet and yet it has no added sugar. Can you explain this?

c Why was the mould wetted before the mixture was added?

Lunch

Lunch is a meal which is often eaten away from home.

- Talk about planning lunches.
- Is your lunch planned and packed at home?
- Do you buy it? If so, do you plan what to buy?

- Do you go home for lunch? Is it ready when you get there?
- How many 'lunch plans' can you identify in your class?
- Does the day of the week make any difference to lunches eaten?

Workshop

1   Next lunchtime carry out a piece of research by **observation** — learning by watching others — in Practical Exercise No. 19.

Practical Exercise No. 19
Lunch Menus

Aim
- To discover how nutritious pupils' lunches might be

Procedure
a   Divide your class into small groups of about 3 or 4. Allot one lunch eating area of the school to each group.

b   Each group should have a pencil and paper. They should eat their lunch at their allotted area. While eating they should take note of what all pupils in that area are eating for lunch.

c   Report results back to class.

d   Put foods eaten into groups of similar foods.

e   Draw a lunch pyramid for your school. Put the foods eaten the most at the bottom, and the foods eaten the least at the top.

Discussion
- Is your pyramid anything like the Healthy Diet Pyramid?
- Can you do anything about helping others to eat a healthy diet?
- Is this method of collecting information about what pupils eat for lunch any better than asking lots of pupils to write down what they ate for lunch, that is, conducting a survey?

2 Create a recipe for a 'Super Sandwich' to pack for your next lunch.

3 Most people should eat more of the foods in the 'Eat Most' group.
Some are listed below. Rearrange the letters to find out what they are.
Write one word to describe all these foods. Why are these foods
important for a healthy you?

a SAPTA   f EABRD
b EWATH   g IRCE
c ATOS   h ERY
d NLESOMIA   i RABN
e EAYRLB   j UOLFR

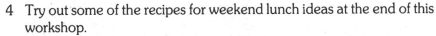

4 Try out some of the recipes for weekend lunch ideas at the end of this
workshop.
How did you like the recipes you tried? Copy the scale below into your
book and put a tick in one of the boxes.

Very Good   Poor

5	4	3	2	1

Give reasons for your rating.

Recipes to Try

Crusty Cheese 'n' Onions

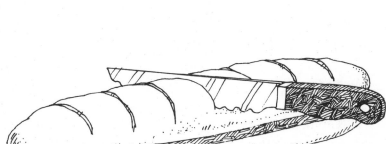

Ingredients

½ French bread stick
½ onion, chopped
50 g margarine
1 tomato
¼ tsp oregano
4 slices mozzarella or Cheddar cheese

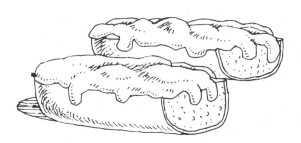

Method

1 Halve French bread stick lengthwise, then cut in half again.

2 Heat 25 g butter or margarine in pan and fry each cut surface until golden brown.

3 Remove bread and heat remaining butter or margarine. Sauté chopped onion until slightly golden brown.

4 Chop tomatoes and mix with onion and oregano. Place onto fried bread.

5 Place cheese on each piece of bread. Place in the oven at 180°C mark 4 for 15–20 minutes.

Serves 2-4 depending on appetite!

Apple Edam Open Sandwich

Place lettuce, then slices of apple and edam cheese on a buttered slice of wholemeal bread. Spoon a little yoghurt or mayonnaise on top and decorate with chopped nuts.

Egg and Bacon Flan

Ingredients

Pastry
50 g flour
25 g margarine
2–3 tsp water

Filling
1 egg
2 tbsp milk
½ tsp chopped parsley
⅓ bacon rasher (25 g)

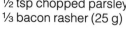

Method

1 Sift flour.

2 Rub in margarine.

3 Add water and mix to a stiff dough. Knead lightly.

4 Roll pastry out to fit a small flan dish (15 cm).

5 Line dish neatly making sure that pastry is not pulled away from the tin. Trim the edge neatly.

6 Mix egg, milk and parsley.

7 Cut bacon into ½ cm squares and place in pastry case. Pour egg mixture over bacon.

8 Place dish on a tray. Bake at 190°C mark 5 for 30 minutes.

Serves 1.

Food and Us

People are of different shapes, different colours and different sizes. But, all people need food and they eat the food that is available in their country.

Some foods are associated with a particular country.

With which country do you associate rice? pasta?

In Britain our diet has been made much more interesting and varied by the introduction of foods from other countries. Chow mein, curry kebabs, pizza and chilli con carne are all familiar dishes to most people. In large towns and cities Chinese, Italian and Indian restaurants are common, while most large supermarkets now stock a wide variety of foreign ingredients and foods. Many foreign meals are much healthier than typically British meals because they contain less meat and more vegetables. Compare these meals to some typically British meals:

Chicken chop suey, boiled rice. (Chinese)
Vegetable curry, chapattis, yoghurt. (Indian)
Pizza, green salad. (Italian)

Ask everyone in your class to write down what they ate for dinner last night.

- Share this information with each other.
- How many different meals were there?
- How many were the same?
- Why do we eat different foods?
- Make a list of these reasons in your book.
- How many people in your class have relatives who were born overseas?
- Discuss how this might influence the foods you eat.

Other things influence what we eat: our friends, the way we feel, the time we have, the money we have, the advertisements we see and hear. (We will look a little further at advertising in the workshop.)

The day of the year might also influence the foods you eat. Think about special days in the year:

Christmas, Birthdays, Divali, Easter, Chinese New Year, Weddings.

- Which special foods do you think of for each of these special days?

- What other special days are there for your family that go with special foods?
- Are there also special days when some foods are not allowed? Why?

Workshop

1 Find out about Christmas in different countries and the foods that go with Christmas. Prepare an International Christmas display in your Home Economics Room.

2 Organise an International Food Day at your school. Prepare a 'feast' and invite others in the school *or* have the 'feast' at the weekend and ask your parents to bring a dish from their region or country of birth and join in the fun.

3 Cook yourself a meat pie. You will find the recipe at the end of this workshop.

4 Practical Exercise No. 20.

Practical Exercise No. 20
Food, Advertising and Me

Aim
- To become aware of food advertisements

Procedure
a Over the period of one week, list all the foods you see and hear advertised on TV, radio, hoardings, newspapers and magazines.

b Underline in green all the advertised foods on your list that you have tasted.

c Describe fully the advertisement for *one* of the foods you underlined.

d Group the foods you listed in the same groups used on the Healthy Diet Pyramid.

Discussion
- Does the advertisement you described fully give you accurate information about the food?

- Which group of foods is advertised the most?

- Why is this group advertised the most?

Food Advertising

5 To bring this section 'A Day with Food' to a close, plan and prepare a dinner in class. Select at least one recipe from another country. There are some recipes here and many more elsewhere in this book.

Recipes to Try

Meat Pies

Ingredients

250 g minced steak
½ diced onion
1 tbsp cornflour
125 ml water
pinch mixed herbs
1 beef stock cube

Pastry

150 g wholemeal flour
150 g plain flour
125 g margarine
100 ml water approximately

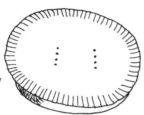

Method

1 Dry fry meat and onions until meat is browned. Add stock cube dissolved in 125 ml boiling water.

2 Simmer the filling for 30 minutes. Thicken mixture by adding cornflour blended to a smooth paste with 1 tbsp cold water, bring to boil, cool.

3 Mix the flours together.

4 Rub margarine into flour with fingertips, keeping the mixture *cool* at all times.

5 When the mixture looks like breadcrumbs, mix it to a stiff dough with *cold* water. Knead a little until the dough is smooth.

This is the Rubbing In method.

Pastry Making Rule — Keep Everything Cool

6 Cut off ⅓ of the dough and put it aside. Roll the rest of the dough out about ½ cm thick.

7 Line the bases of 4 meat pie tins, or one large plate.

8 Place ¼ of the filling into each pastry case.

9 Roll out the remaining pastry to ½ cm thick.

10 Brush the edge of the pastry in the tin with water. Cover each pie with pastry, press edges and trim with a knife.

11 Make one or two holes in top of pastry with a skewer.

● What are the holes for?

12 Glaze the top of each pie with egg glaze.

13 Place pie tins on a tray and put in the top of a hot oven for 20-25 minutes to cook pastry and heat up meat.

Make 4 small pies, or one large one.

● What is the temperature of a *hot* oven? See page 10 if you need help.

More Pastry Making Rules

● bake it hot

● do not open for at least 10 mins or your pastry will f
l
o
p

Samosas (Indian)

Ingredients

Pastry
225 g plain flour
4 tbsp vegetable oil
4–6 tbsp water

Filling
200 g cooked mashed potato
50 g peas
50 g cooked diced carrot
1 onion (grated)
pinch curry powder

Method

1 Make filling by mixing all vegetables together and adding curry powder.

2 Make pastry: Sieve flour into mixing bowl, add oil and mix with a fork until the mixture resembles breadcrumbs. Add water gradually to make a firm dough.

3 Turn dough onto a floured worksurface and knead until smooth.

4 Divide mixture into 10 balls. Roll each ball into a circle, cut circle in half. Make a cone shape with the semi-circle, seal the join with water or flour and water paste.

5 Fill cone shapes with vegetable mixture and seal the top. See diagrams.

6 Cook Samosas in 5cm of vegetable oil, turning until golden brown all over, drain on kitchen paper serve immediately.

Rules for Deep Fat Frying

a Dry food before putting into hot oil.

b Do not over heat the oil – control the heat carefully.

c The pan should not be more than half full of oil.

d Lower food gently and carefully into the hot oil using the basket or a draining spoon.

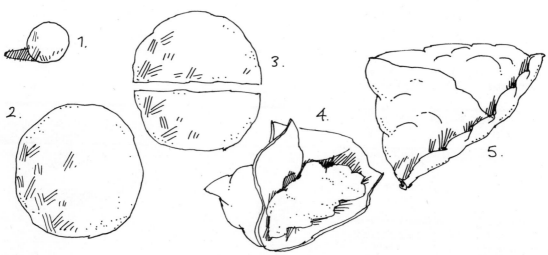

Chicken Chop Suey (Chinese)
(Stir-fry chicken and mixed vegetables)

Ingredients

250 g boneless chicken
1 onion
100 g bean sprouts
50 g mushrooms
1 small carrot
soy sauce
1 tbsp vegetable oil
optional: water chestnuts, bamboo shoots, chinese leaves

Method

1 Cut chicken into small pieces, slice onion into thin rings, wash and slice mushrooms, peel carrot and cut into thin slices.

2 Fry chicken and onion in a small amount of vegetable oil for 10 minutes until chicken is cooked.

3 Add the rest of the vegetables and cook for another 5 minutes stirring all the time.

4 Add a little soy sauce. Serve with boiled rice

Serves 2–3.

Moussaka (Greek)

Ingredients

1 aubergine
1 tbsp vegetable oil
1 onion chopped
125 g minced beef or lamb
1 slice wholemeal bread (made into breadcrumbs)
1 tbsp tomato purée
1 tsp herbs
pepper
Cheese sauce; 250 ml skimmed milk
100 g low fat Cheddar cheese
1 rounded tbsp cornflour

Method

1 Wash aubergines, cut into ½cm slices, fry gently in oil for 15 minutes.

2 Dry fry meat until fat runs out, drain off any excess fat.

3 Add onion, purée, herbs, breadcrumbs and 125 ml of water to meat. Leave to simmer for 20 minutes.

4 Make cheese sauce: put cornflour into a saucepan, gradually blend in the milk. Bring to the boil stirring continually until the sauce boils and thickens. Stir in grated cheese.

5 Put aubergines in the bottom of a dish, spread meat mixture over them and finish with a layer of cheese sauce. Bake for 30 minutes 190°C mark 5.

Serves 2.

Part 3   Evaluation Test

1 Unscramble the following **food preparation** words.

a	OHCP	g	NKEDA
b	CIDE	h	EFEZRE
c	REDSH	i	XIM
d	RIST	j	ZGALE
e	AGRET	k	ELEP
f	ABET	l	EASRDP

2 Unscramble the following **cooking method** words.

a	IOLB	g	OSRAT
b	ISMEMR	h	KABE
c	RFY	i	EASTM
d	LIRLG	j	OASTT
e	ROWBN	k	AUSTE
f	RCUEBABE	l	WEST

3 Different foods have different uses in the body. Some ways in which the body uses food are listed below. Sketch and label three foods needed by the body for each use.

a Keep bones and teeth strong.

b Keep the body growing and repairing.

c Supply the body with energy.

4 Which of the foods listed below, according to the Healthy Diet Pyramid, does the body need the most to keep healthy?
fats,   milk,   eggs,   cereals,   fruit,   oils,
vegetables,   meat,   nuts

5 Make up a healthy school lunch menu for yourself and show how it 'fits' the Healthy Diet Pyramid by putting the foods you use in the correct columns.

Menu:

Eat the most of these foods	Eat these foods moderately	Eat the least of these foods

6 a

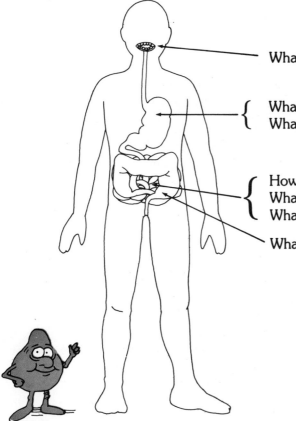

What happens to food in the mouth?

{ What is this called?
  What happens to food here?

{ How long is this?
  What is it called?
  What happens to food here?

What goes into the blood from here?

b What does the drawing above represent: the excretory system, the respiratory system, the digestive system, or the circulatory system? Write the correct answer in your book.

7 a Why is fibre an important part of your diet?

   b The following is a list of ingredients for a recipe. Write *all* the ingredients that contain fibre in your book.
   120 g wholemeal flour   25 g unprocessed bran
   75 g S.R. flour   1 egg
   1 grated apple   250 ml yoghurt

8 a Why is breakfast an important meal?

   b Which of the following breakfast menus would be the healthiest one for you?
   Menu 1: cornflakes, sliced banana and milk; ½ buttered wholemeal roll; glass of milk.
   Menu 2: porridge and milk; fried egg and bacon; 1 slice white toast + butter + marmalade; cup of tea.
   Menu 3: 2 slices white toast + butter + marmalade + Marmite; cup of coffee.

9   List five healthy snacks you could serve at your next birthday party.

10 Copy this drawing of the tooth into your book.
    a   Label the shaded parts.
    b   Draw an arrow pointing to the parts of the tooth most likely to develop holes.
    c   How do holes form in teeth?
    d   Which foods are most likely to cause holes to develop in teeth?
    e   How can you help to prevent holes developing in your teeth? List three ways.

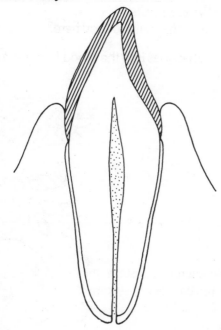

11 a   List four things that might influence which foods you eat.
    b   Write as much as you can about one of the influences you listed above.

Part 4   About Me

10　Looking at Me

What makes you *you*?

Your nose?　　　Your walk?

Your voice?　　　Your name?

Your smile?

The way you look is the result of a mixture of Dad's looks and Mum's looks.

MUM'S FRECKLES

DAD'S HAIR

MUM'S EYES

DAD'S TEETH

MIXTURE OF MUM'S & DAD'S BODY BUILD

MUM'S HAIR

DAD'S NOSE

MUM'S EYES

MIXTURE OF MUM'S & DADS SKIN COLOUR

DAD'S BODY BUILD

These looks are decided before you are born and cannot be changed.

But what about the way you talk, walk and act? You learn to do these things by copying others, so you tend to speak, walk and act like the adult(s) you were with when you were a very small child. *But* there will always be differences that make the way you walk, talk and act especially *you*.

You are given a name which is your very own. This helps other people to remember you and it helps you to recognise the things that belong to you.

● Why do many people have *two* first names?

You also own lots of different things.

● Discuss the things that belong to you that make you feel special when you say "My ...." (e.g. My dog).

Many things make you especially you, but you are also similar to others in lots of ways.

● Discuss the ways people are similar, e.g. the position of noses. Make a list of these similarities on the board or in your book.

Workshop

1　Copy the list of things describing you below into your book. Beside each item, put a **D** if it is describing a part of you that was **decided** before you were born, and an **L** if it is something you have **learned** somehow.

　a　The shape of your nose ....

　b　The way you walk ....

　c　Ability to run well ....

　d　Being a responsible person ....

　e　The colour of your eyes ....

f   Your height ....
g   The way you dress ....
h   The colour of your skin ....
i   The colour of your hair ....
j   The way you talk ....

2   Can you think of something that is yours and only yours and no one else's is the same?
If you are stumped look to the right for help!

3   What does your name mean? Look it up in a book of names in the library.
Are you like the meaning of your name?

FINGERPRINTS

Practical Exercise No. 21
Understanding Me

Aim
● To help me to understand myself a little better

Procedure
a   Collect the ingredients for the recipe at the end of this workshop.

b   Prepare the recipe on your own. If you run out of ideas look around the class for help.

c   When the whole class is finished, place all the results together on one table.

d   Look at everyone's work, then answer the following questions:
— If your salad is different from anyone else's, how is it different?
— Were all your arrangements your own ideas?
— Did you 'borrow' some ideas from others? List these.
(Remember we said earlier that we learn from others.)

Evaluation
● Did this exercise help you to understand yourself a little better? If so write a sentence in your book explaining how.

● If you do not think this exercise helped you to understand yourself a little better, explain why your salad looked the way it did.

Recipes to Try

My Salad

Ingredients

½ tomato
1 slice pineapple
1 slice wholemeal bread
1 slice white bread
2 tsp butter or margarine
1 slice *or* 1 portion of cheese
1 lettuce leaf
1-2 pieces celery
1 slice meat
1 slice orange
1 spring onion
1 small piece cucumber

Method

1 Read through the list of salad ingredients and choose a selection of those ingredients which you would like for your salad.

 Remember: Salads provide us with fibre, vitamins and water; and the meat, cheese or egg we add to it give us protein for growth and repair.

2 Select a dinner plate.

3 Wash all salad vegetables and cut as desired.

4 Arrange *your own* individual salad. Work quickly and neatly.

Questions about the recipe

a Salads usually include vegetables and maybe fruit, and are served with some meat or cheese or egg. Why?

b At which time of the year do we often eat salads. Why?

11   People and Me

Friends

What makes a friend a friend?
Her hobbies?
His laughter?
His honesty?
Her manners?

- What are the things you like about people?
- Make a list of these things in your book.

Most of us *need* other people to:

- care about
- share with
- talk to
- eat with
- understand us
- be with.

Friends are people who meet some of these **needs**.

You know a lot of people. Not all of them are friends. Some are just acquaintances.

- What is the difference between a **friend** and an **acquaintance**?

Workshop

1   Read the following story. In your book, make a list of all the actions in the story that would be made by a friend, and another list of all the actions that would *not* be made by a friend.

David and Joan walked to school together. Mary would not wait because she was afraid she would be late. Just as they got to school David slipped and fell on the wet concrete. One girl laughed at him and another called him 'dummy'. Joan helped him up and picked up the books he dropped. They hurried on to class.

Joe bumped into them in the corridor and rushed on. David's pencil was gone. He asked James if he could borrow one, but James said, "No, my extra one is brand new". Anica loaned him one.

David and Joan had lunch together. They sat with a new boy who was alone. Jill came up and poked David, saying "How could you be so careless and rip your jeans?" Joan stuck up for him and said that the concrete was very slippery because it was wet.

Mary joined them on the way home but she wanted to take a new route home or she wouldn't walk with them.

2 Make (or just design) a poster advertising yourself as a friend.

3 Write out an advertisement for an imaginary newspaper, starting with "Friend wanted, must be....."

4 Practical Exercise No. 22.

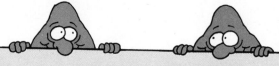

Practical Exercise No. 22
Friendship

Aim
- To help me to understand the meaning of friendship

Procedure

a Your teacher may divide the class into groups of four.

b As a group plan a simple meal. Use the recipes in this book or the ones your teacher gives you. (Menus are suggested at the end of this workshop.)

c As a group plan how you will manage the menu. (The lesson about friends and this planning could be done in one session and the meal prepared the next session.)
No decision should be made without *all* members of your group having their say. Make notes to guide yourselves and do not forget the time limit for your class.

d While you work at preparing your menu, remember all the things you like about people that you listed in class. Attempt to put these things into action.

e Any decisions to be made during preparation of food must only be made after *every* member of your group has had his/her say.

Discussion

- Did you enjoy the activity?
- Is it easier working in a group than by yourself?
- Did one member of the group make more decisions than the rest?
- Think back to the beginning of this chapter. What things did you consider important about a friend?
- How did each member of your group rate as a friend?
  Excellent   Very Good   Good   Fair   Poor
- How do you think you rated as a friend?
  Excellent   Very Good   Good   Fair   Poor

Suggested Menus:

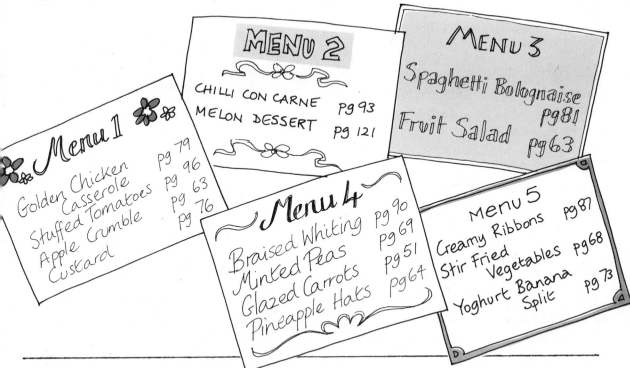

Menu 2

CHILLI CON CARNE   Pg 93

MELON DESSERT   Pg 121

Menu 3

Spaghetti Bolognaise   Pg 81

Fruit Salad   Pg 63

Menu 1

Golden Chicken Casserole   Pg 79

Stuffed Tomatoes   Pg 96

Apple Crumble   Pg 63

Custard   Pg 76

Menu 4

Braised Whiting   Pg 90

Minted Peas   Pg 69

Glazed Carrots   Pg 51

Pineapple Hats   Pg 64

Menu 5

Creamy Ribbons   Pg 87

Stir Fried Vegetables   Pg 68

Yoghurt Banana Split   Pg 73

The Community

As a baby you most likely started out life with your parents and, maybe, brothers and sisters. As you grew, you started to meet people in the baby clinic, play groups, the street, the shops, the schools. These places make up your community. Communities like your town or suburb make up the society in which we all live.

British Society

Individual

Family

Birds, animals, fish and human beings tend to live together in groups. Your community is made up of groups of people, the most common group being the **family** group.

Most groups formed *outside* the family group have an interest in common, for example, sports, gardens, country of origin.

- How many different groups can you think of in your community?
- How many of these groups do you belong to? Are any of these groups found throughout the country? (e.g. Scouts and Guides)

The community in which you live provides **resources** which are shared by many people.

A **resource** is something you use to do the things you need or want to do. Some of these community resources are jumbled here.

- Can you think of more?
- Could you provide any of these resources for yourself and your family?
- What does your family give to your community?
- What does your community give to your family?
- How could your family and community relationships be improved?

BANKS
SHOP
FOOTBALL
SWIMMING POOL
SCHOOL
CHURCH
FOOD
DOCTOR
PAPER
HOSPITAL
TRAINS
ROADS
LIBRARY
FIRE BRIGADE
INSURANCE
ROADS

Workshop

1 With your teacher's assistance organise a class buffet.
   List the resources you will need to do this.
   Organise class members to bring food for the buffet.
   - Could you organise a buffet in your community to bring people together? Discuss a suitable occasion to celebrate.

2 If you live in a city, organise through your teacher to write to pupils at a small country school. Discover through your letters how community resources might differ in the two areas, e.g. some areas might have a mobile library.
   Or, if you live in a country town or community, organise the above activity by writing to pupils in a city.

3 Visit one of your local community resources to find out what services it provides and who uses it, e.g. the local library or swimming pool.

4 As a class make up a community pot of soup — everyone in your 'community' (class) should prepare a part of the soup — that is, help in a community activity. The class can then share the soup when it is cooked.

Minestrone Soup

Ingredients

75 g lentils
1 tbsp vegetable oil
2 chopped onions
2 cloves garlic (crushed)
2½ litres water
3 carrots, diced
2 sticks celery, sliced
2 diced potatoes
75 g sliced green beans
3 sliced courgettes
4 tomatoes, chopped
50 g small macaroni
2 tbsp parsley, chopped
Parmesan cheese (optional)

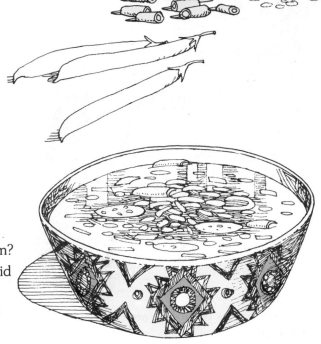

Method

1 Heat oil in large saucepan, add onions and garlic. Sauté until onions are transparent.

2 Add water and lentils. Cover and simmer for 15 minutes.

3 Add vegetables, simmer for ¾ hour. Add macaroni and simmer for a further 10-15 minutes.

4 Stir in parsley and serve sprinkled with cheese.

Serves class of 20.

Questions about the recipe

a Which country does this recipe come from?

b On which part of the Healthy Diet Pyramid do *most* of the ingredients belong?

c When is the best time to serve a thick rich soup like this one?

Family

When we looked at the Clarke family in Chapter 1, we decided that many families in the world are similar. In the previous section we talked about families being the most common group in our community.

● What are the differences between the family group and other groups?

Families can be called **primary** (first) groups. They are groups in which the members care for one another.

Secondary groups are ones in which people may share interests such as horseriding or photography. But you are generally not as close to these people as you usually are to your family group.

Primary Group

Secondary Group

Your family is the group you are born into or adopted into.

A family is important because it meets the many needs you have throughout your life.

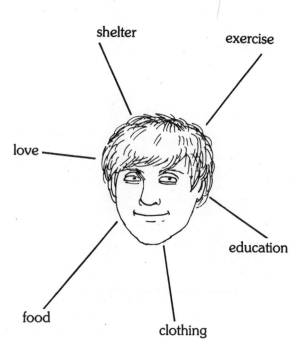

shelter

exercise

love

education

food

clothing

● Are there any other needs you have that your family meets?

There are many different types of families throughout the world.

In Britain the most common type of family is the **nuclear** family.

A nuclear family is made up of one or both parents and children living together. Some families may be made up of the father, mother and their children, as well as the grandparents or other relatives. This is called an **extended** family.

● Why is it called an extended family?

Remember: Every family is different.

Families differ in the
— number of people they have in them
— resources they have, such as housing, money, skills (the things they can do)
— things that they want.

- Discuss how families are different in the things they have, are able to do, and want.

- Make a list of the things your family does for you.
- Make a list of the things that you do for your family.
- How could you help more at home?
- How could your family help you a little more?

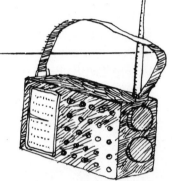

Workshop

1 Below are three lists. Each list has lost its heading. The headings and their meanings are here:

Heading	Meaning
Survival Needs	The things I must have to survive
Secondary Needs	The things I need to live a happy healthy life but could probably survive without
Wants	Things not necessary to my survival

Copy these lists into your book and choose the correct heading for each.

....	....	....
Food	Radio	Friends
Shelter	Bicycle	Soap
Clothing	Fashion Clothing	Education
Sleep	Grilled Steak	Family
Exercise	Tennis Racquet	Love
Other People	Wristwatch	Fresh Fruit

2 Write a letter to a family overseas. In your letter talk about your family and your community.

3 Bring a favourite recipe from home and help to make up a Family Recipe Book for your class.

4 Choose some recipes brought to class and in 'family' groups of four, prepare a healthy meal. Add any new Home Economics words to your glossary.

5 How has Home Economics helped you to manage family living?

12   Exploring Needs

Shelter

When you were little did you ever build a den or play games about houses?
Where did you build this shelter? In a tree? Against a fence? Under the dining room table? In your bedroom?
Have you ever watched children play house? Did anyone ever give you a play tent for your birthday?

- Discuss the reasons why man needs shelter.

- Who might live in each of the houses or shelters on this page?

- Why are there different types of houses in different parts of the world?

- Why are there different types of houses in the same town?

Whatever the type of shelter we choose to live under, it provides us with:
— privacy
— protection from the weather
— comfort
— a setting for our development and the development of our families.

We call this shelter **home**. We fill our home with our possessions and usually share it with our family and/or our friends.
One regular activity in a home is the preparation of the food a family needs to keep healthy.

- How might the resources available in a home (e.g. storage, preparation resources, money) influence the food eaten?

Workshop

1   Look at the drawings of the types of shelter. See if you can name each type of housing.

144

2 Practical Exercise No. 23.

Practical Exercise No. 23
Home Resources

Aim
- To prepare a healthy meal for two (or four) people with only one gas jet burner or one hotplate available for cooking

Procedure
a Select recipes for a 2-course healthy meal. A menu is suggested at the end of this workshop, or you may wish to make up your own menu.

b Read the recipes through carefully.

c Plan your meal preparation on one gas burner or one hotplate so that the meal will be served in the limited time available to the class.

d Make sure that both courses are served up on time.

e — Where do you think home might be when you have only one gas burner or hotplate for cooking?

   — Plan another healthy meal cooked on one burner. Use recipes from other lessons.

Chicken Risotto

Ingredients

100 g brown rice
pinch mixed herbs
1 onion
50 g peas
50 g sweetcorn
150-200 g boned chicken
1 chicken stock cube
1 tbsp vegetable oil

Extras, small quantities of the following may also be added, mushrooms, celery, red or green peppers.

Method

1 Chop onion and chicken.

2 Fry onion and chicken in the oil, add rice, cook for 3 minutes.

3 Add stock cube dissolved in 250 ml boiling water.

4 Simmer gently for 15 minutes.

5 Add vegetables, simmer for a further 15–20 minutes until rice is cooked.

6 Stir occasionally and add more water if necessary.

Serves 2.

Pear Mouse

Quantity		Ingredients
For 4 people	For 2 people	
2	1	firm cooking pear(s)
a 4 cm piece	a 2 cm piece	cinnamon stick
500 ml	375 ml	water
4 pieces	2 pieces	liquorice laces (for tail)
few drops	few drops	pink colouring
1 tbsp	2 tsp	sugar (optional)
4	2	almond kernels
12	6	whole cloves

Method

1 Peel pear neatly. Cut in half lengthwise and carefully remove core with a teaspoon.

2 Place sugar (optional), water and cinnamon stick into a saucepan and bring to the boil.

3 Add pear halves to liquid and simmer until tender (about 10 minutes).

4 Remove pear from syrup into a serving dish (preferably glass).

5 When cool enough to handle, make pear into a mouse by splitting the almond for two ears, using the cloves for eyes and nose, and the liquorice for a tail.

6 Colour the syrup pale pink and discard the cinnamon stick. Pour a little syrup around the mouse. Serve.

Warmth

It makes no difference whether you feel hot or cold, your body temperature (i.e. the temperature of your blood) stays at 37°C, unless you are ill or unless you are exposed to heat or cold for a long time, without being suitably dressed.

Your body works best if your temperature is 37°C. You help to keep this temperature constant with the clothes you wear, the shelter you select for living and the work your body does. Clothes, shelter and food for energy are **survival needs.**

- How do you keep warm in winter?

Your skin helps to regulate the amount of warmth in your body and keeps your blood temperature steady all the year round. Having a constant body temperature means that you can live in very cold or very hot climates.

- Which parts of the world are very hot? Which parts are very cold?

Heat is a by-product of the breakdown of food to produce mechanical energy. This energy is used for moving about, writing, keeping all parts of your body working — even your brain, when you are reading this, is using part of your last meal to provide the energy it needs. *All* foods that supply energy produce heat when they are broken down. The energy-rich foods contain carbohydrate or fat.

- Which is best for providing heat, a hot cup of tea or an ice-cold milk shake? Why?

When you are using energy for running, heat is produced. Your blood temperature stays at 37°C, any heat you do not need you get rid of through the skin or through your breath.

When you turn an oven on you have a thermostat to regulate the heat. In your body your brain acts as the thermostat. If your blood temperature rises above or drops below 37°C, the brain sends messages to the skin and other parts of the body to put it right.

Workshop

1 Find out the air temperature range throughout the year in Britain and in Jamaica. If one individual from each country packed all his/her clothing into cases, whose clothes do you think would take up the most room? Explain your answer.

2 There are two recipes at the end of this workshop. Do you think one recipe is more suitable for summer and one for winter? Remember what you have read on this page — but also think about how you *feel* when you eat food.

3 Try the recipe that *feels* right for the season you are experiencing now.

Recipes to Try

Pasties

Ingredients

75 g plain flour
75 g wholemeal flour
75 g margarine
6–8 tsps cold water.

Method

1 Sift flour into a mixing bowl.
2 Rub margarine into flour with fingertips until mixture looks like breadcrumbs.
3 Gradually add enough water to mix to a firm dough.
4 Sprinkle board lightly with flour, turn dough onto board and knead lightly until smooth.
5 Divide pastry into 2 even-sized pieces and shape each into a round.

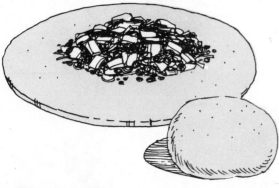

Filling Ingredients

100 g minced steak
½ potato
¼ small onion
¼ small turnip
a few shakes of pepper and salt (optional)
¼ medium carrot
2 tsp chopped parsley
Note: Vegetarians might like to replace the meat in this recipe with 100 g baked beans or 100 g diced cheese.

Method

1 Dice potato, turnip and onion. Grate carrot.
2 Mix all filling ingredients together.
3 Roll each piece of pastry into a round the size of a saucer.
4 Place an equal portion of filling onto each round, brush the edges of the pastry with water and join over the top of the mixture. Pinch edges together.

5 Place on a greased baking tray, prick the top with a fork. Glaze with egg and water.

6 Place in a hot oven (220°C mark 7) for 10–15 minutes then move tray to the middle shelf for a further 15 minutes. (Someone else can then use the shelf above.)

Questions about the recipe

a What method of mixing is used for the pastry?
b Can you suggest why you need to make holes in the top of your pastry before baking?
c How many parts of the Healthy Diet Pyramid are represented in a pasty? Which part of the pyramid is best represented?
d What are the rules for pastry making you saw earlier in this book? (See p. 127 if you need help.)

Super Potato Salad

Ingredients

3 medium-sized potatoes
2 slices ham
50 g cooked peas
4 spring onions
1 gherkin
1 can sardines *or* 2 hard-boiled eggs
60 g cheddar cheese
100 ml mayonnaise (low fat)
4 lettuce leaves — washed and crisp
1 pear

Method

1 Peel potatoes, cut in half. Cover with water, add a pinch of salt and simmer for 15-20 minutes or until tender.

2 Drain potatoes and dice into 1½ cm cubes. Spread out on a plate to cool.

3 Cut ham into thin strips.

4 Slice onion finely.

5 Dice gherkin finely.

6 Grate cheese.

7 Place a lettuce leaf on each serving dish.

8 Gently fold all ingredients together except ham, sardines (or egg) and pear.

9 Open can of sardines and drain oil. Place sardines on paper towel to absorb excess oil (or peel shell from eggs and cut into slices).

10 Pile potato salad onto lettuce. Place sardines (or egg) on top and criss-cross with strips of ham.

11 Peel pear, remove core and cut into 4-8 sections. Garnish salad with pear. Chill and serve.

Serves 4.

To hard-boil an egg:

Place the egg into a saucepan and cover with *cold* water. Place on the heat and bring to the boil quickly for 10 minutes. Remove the egg and immediately run it under cold water and crack the shell to prevent a greyish layer forming over the yolk.

Questions about the recipe

a To which part of the Healthy Diet Pyramid do most of the ingredients belong?

b Find out how each of the vegetables in the recipe grows.

c How many other ways can you cook a potato?

d Why did we peel and slice the pear only at the last minute?
Answer **e** *or* **f**.

e Why should you crack the shell of a hard-boiled egg and cool it quickly as soon as it is cooked?

f Why should you drain sardines on absorbent paper before using?

Sleep

- How long do you sleep each night?
- How does this compare with others in your class at school?
- Conduct a brief survey: Ask each person how long he/she slept last night. Record the results on the board. What is the most common amount of sleeping time for members of your class?

You can last longer without food than you can without sleep. In fact you spend about ⅓ of your life sleeping.

Each person needs a different amount of sleep, but teenagers probably need 8-10 hours each night.

If you miss some of your sleep one day then you are able to 'catch up' the next day by sleeping longer than usual.

While you sleep your body activities have a chance to slow down, and your muscles can relax. The whole body rests.

Sleep is one of your survival needs. Without enough sleep you are unable to carry out the day's tasks and you are more likely to become ill.

Exercise

Exercise is another survival need.
You have been given a body that has been built to be exercised.
Just to see to your everyday needs you must exercise — you exercise while walking to school, while cleaning your teeth or while eating your meals.

Some people go beyond everyday exercise and enjoy playing football or tennis, or going for a swim.

- Discuss the ways people exercise.

Your muscles like to be exercised; without exercise they become slack and your joints become stiff. Exercise keeps your muscles firm and your joints working like the well-oiled hinges of a door.

Your digestive system and your blood system also work better in a healthy, well-exercised body. . . Don't forget that the heart is a muscle. Without exercise your muscles will 'age'.

Do you need to exercise more? If you do, how can you do this?

Workshop

1 Find out how many sporting and recreation areas there are in your community. How many of these do you use?

2 a Prepare a healthy snack for an active person that will help keep the inside of the digestive system healthy and provide a lot of energy. There are some suitable recipes at the end of this workshop.

   b How well did the recipe you used 'fit' the Healthy Diet Pyramid?

   c Which of the ingredients you used in your recipe help to keep the inside of the digestive system healthy? How do they do this?

   d Which of the ingredients in the recipe you used are a source of energy?

Recipes to Try

Pizza Towers

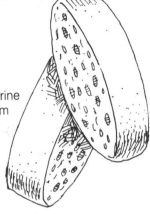

Ingredients

4 crumpets
25 g butter or margarine
4 slices salami or ham
4 slices tomato
4 slices pineapple
50 g grated cheese

Method

1 Butter hot toasted crumpets.

2 Place salami or ham on each crumpet and heat under grill.

3 Place tomato on each salami slice and place under grill.

4 Place pineapple on each tomato slice and place under grill.

5 Top with cheese and place under grill again until cheese melts.

Serves 4.

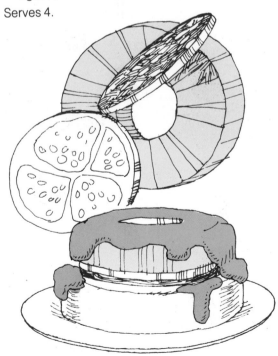

Muffin, Cheese and Egg Sandwiches

Ingredients

2 wholemeal muffins or rolls
25 g butter or margarine
2 hard-boiled eggs (place egg in cold water, bring to the boil for 10 minutes)
100 g grated cheese
1 tbsp tomato sauce
25 g finely diced celery

Method

1 Split muffins, toast under grill and spread with butter.

2 Top with slices of hard-boiled egg.

3 Mix cheese, celery and sauce together and sprinkle over egg.

4 Place under grill to melt cheese.

Serves 4.

Apple, Marshmallow Magic

Ingredients

2 fruit teacakes
100 g cooked apple
8 marshmallows
1 tsp lemon juice
pinch cinnamon
2 tsp coconut

Method

1 Split teacakes and toast them.

2 Mix apple, chopped marshmallows, lemon juice and cinnamon together.

3 Cover surface of teacakes with apple mixture. Place under grill until marshmallow begins to melt.

4 Sprinkle with coconut and place back under grill until golden brown.

Serves 4.

Part 4   Evaluation Test

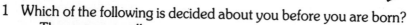

1   Which of the following is decided about you before you are born?
    a   The way you walk
    b   The way you dress
    c   The colour of your eyes
    d   The way you talk

2   Which of the following is the same in most people?
    a   The colour of the skin
    b   The ability to run
    c   Height
    d   The parts of the face

3   Write a sentence explaining what is important about friendship.

4   Explain the difference between a family and a community.

5   List 5 ways in which familes might be different.

6   Which of the following are survival needs?
    Exercise   Love   Food   Sleep   Radio   Friends   Clothing
    Other People   Family   Shelter   Education   Soap

7   Write a sentence explaining why man needs shelter.

8   What are the two main parts of the body that regulate our body temperature? Explain how these work together.

9   Why is sleep important for good health?

10 How does exercise improve the way the body works?

(Teachers might wish to add questions about the recipes used.)

Find Your Way To Health

Follow the Good Health Trail to a healthy you!

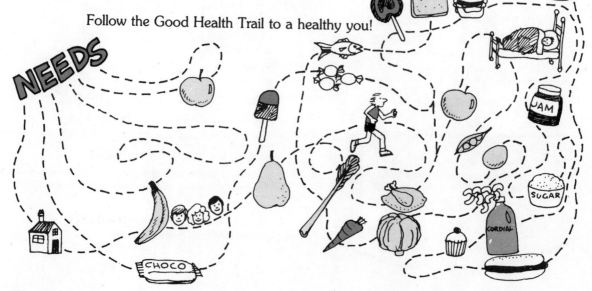

Puzzle Answers

Page 4

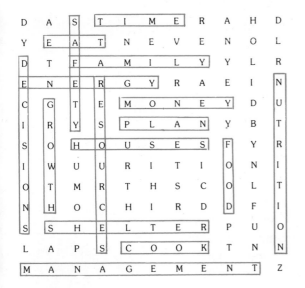

Page 16

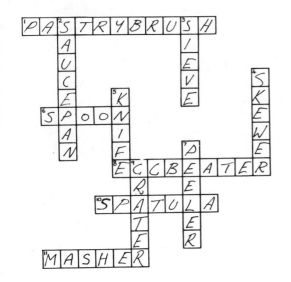

Page 32

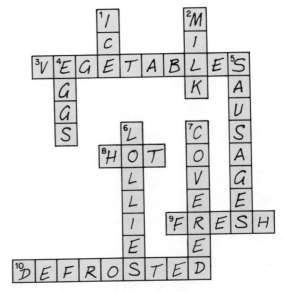

Page 38

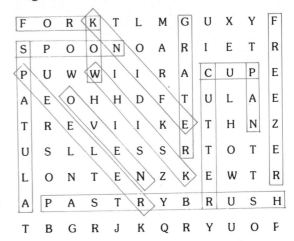

Page 43

Food is anything that you eat that your body can use.

```
A D E F O O D A
T H I S S N O T
A N Y T H I N G
T S T H A T O E
Y O U M U E A T
T H A T A S T E
E Y O U R T E A
B O D Y T C A N
A U U S E M O S
```

Page 47

healthy diet

Page 55

a oats
b wheat
c rye
d corn
e flour
f rice
g bread
h rolled oats

i cornflour
j pasta
k barley
l bran
m maize
n cornflakes
o wholemeal flour

Page 58

Scotland, Mexico, India, Lebanon, Germany, England

Page 62

Citrus Fruits: orange, lime, grapefruit, lemon, mandarin, tangerine, cumquat
Seed Fruits: apples, quince, pear, crab-apples
Vine Fruits: grape, watermelon, honey dew, rockmelon, Kiwi fruit, passionfruit
Stone Fruits: peaches, plums, cherries, nectarines
Berry Fruits: strawberries, blackberries, red currants, loganberries, blueberries, cranberries

Sub-tropical and Tropical Fruits: figs, banana, paw paw, mango, lychee, pomegranate, dates, pineapple, persimmon

Page 66

- a lettuce
  b cabbage
  c celery
  d beansprouts
  e asparagus
  f beans

  g peas
  h potatoes
  i onions
  j carrots
  k marrow
  l broccoli

- Shoots — beansprouts
  Stalks — celery, asparagus
  Leaves — lettuce, cabbage
  Flowers — broccoli
  Seeds — beans, peas
  Fruit — marrow
  Bulbs — onions
  Tubers — potatoes
  Roots — carrots

Page 72

- butter, yoghurt, milk, cheese, skimmed milk, cheese, cream, flavoured milk, ice-cream

```
S A U C E S U M S
O Y J U N K E T C
U B I S C U I T O
P A S T A T A T N
S I C A K E S A E
N J O R B R E A D
P L E Q U I C H E
Q M S D R I N K S
```

Page 73

a Brie
b Cheddar
c Stilton
d cottage
e Cheshire
f Edam

g blue vein
h Wensleydale
i Parmesan
j Mozzarella
k Gouda
l Camembert

Page 82

goose, turkey, quail, duck

Page 94

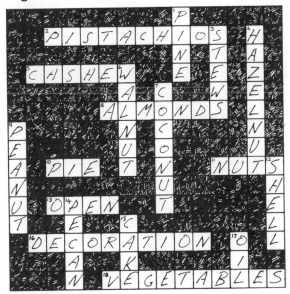

Page 130

- a chop
  b dice
  c shred
  d stir
  e grate
  f beat
  g knead
  h freeze
  i mix
  j glaze
  k peel
  l spread

- a boil
  b simmer
  c fry
  d grill
  e brown
  f barbecue
  g roast
  h bake
  i steam
  j toast
  k sauté
  l stew

Page 135
fingerprints

Page 98
a peanut
b maize
c safflower
d sunflower
e sesame
f soyabean

Page 99

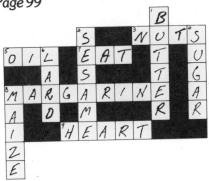

Page 114
wheat, barley, rye, oats, rice

Page 123
a pasta
b wheat
c oats
d semolina
e barley
f bread
g rice
h rye
i bran
j flour

Glossary

Accompaniment a food that is traditionally served with another food, e.g. apple sauce with roast pork

Appliance a piece of equipment used in food preparation that has a power source, e.g. cooker, or an electric whisk

Bake cook in an oven

Beat mix quickly with a fork, egg whisk, whisk or spoon

Blend mix dry and liquid ingredients together until smooth

Boil heat until bubbles rise from the surface of the liquid

Braise cook meat or fish on a bed of vegetables

Buffet food placed on a table and people serve themselves

Cream beat butter and sugar together until they look like cream

Dough a flour and liquid mixture than can be kneaded

Essence liquid flavouring added to food

Evaluation the last step in making a decision, when you decide if you did the right thing, or how well you did it

Fold mix with a plastic scraper or with a spatula, using a cutting motion

Garnish decorate

Glaze brush with liquid to encourage browning in oven

Grill cook under a hot grill until brown or tender

Herbs leaves and stems of plants that give a particular flavour to foods

Malnutrition not enough food or too much of the wrong foods, leading to poor health

Mash break food up with a fork or masher, e.g. potato, until free of lumps

Mix combine ingredients together

Obesity being 20% overweight for height, age and sex

Parboil boil food in water until partly cooked

Pasta all of the foods from the spaghetti family

Peel remove skin of a food

Poach cook gently in hot liquid

Pulses dried peas, beans and lentils also called legumes

Purée mix cooked food through a sieve, or place in a blender

Rasher a slice of bacon

Resource something you use to do the things you need or want

Rind skin of citrus fruits like oranges and lemons

Roast cook in fat in the oven

Roux equal quantities of fat and flour that are cooked together until smooth and used for thickening sauces

Sauté fry lightly in a little butter or margarine

Seasoning salt, pepper, herbs or spices used to give flavour to a food

Shortening fat such as butter or margarine

Simmer heat liquid until surface moves — bubbles do not rise through the surface

Spices seeds, berries, leaves of plants that have distinct flavours and are used whole or ground to give flavour to food

Sprig a small branch of a leafy plant, e.g. parsley

Steam cook over a boiling water bath so that steam rises up through food to cook it

Stew cook food in its own juices with very little or no additional liquid

Stir fry   fry food for a few minutes in very little oil, stirring with a large spoon or spatula, as in Chinese cooking

Survey   a method of finding out what people think, what they have and what they do

Synthetic   not from a plant or animal; man-made, e.g. plastic

Whip   beat lightly with a whisk

Wok   a semi-circular cooking vessel used for stir frying

Recipe Index